KRISHNA HARI

KRISHNA HARI

A Play

by

NANDLAL TULSIRAM

MOTILAL BANARSIDASS PUBLISHERS
PRIVATE LIMITED • DELHI

First Edition: Delhi, 1992

ISBN: 81-208-1055-4

Also available at:
MOTILAL BANARSIDASS
41 U.A., Bungalow Road, Jawahar Nagar, Delhi 110 007
120 Royapettah High Road, Mylapore, Madras 600 004
16 St. Mark's Road, Bangalore 560 001
Ashok Rajpath, Patna 800 004
Chowk, Varanasi 221 001

PRINTED IN INDIA
BY JAINENDRA PRAKASH JAIN AT SHRI JAINENDRA PRESS, A-45 NARAINA INDUSTRIAL AREA, PHASE I, NEW DELHI 110 028 AND PUBLISHED BY NARENDRA PRAKASH JAIN FOR MOTILAL BANARSIDASS PUBLISHERS PVT. LTD., BUNGALOW ROAD, JAWAHAR NAGAR, DELHI 110 007

To my wife

GOMATHI TULSIRAM

ACKNOWLEDGEMENTS

My thanks are due to many individuals who have helped me in writing *Krishna Hari*.

I owe a debt of gratitude to all my children for encouraging and inspiring me to write *Krishna Hari*. Incidentally, Jyoti, my daughter, produced and directed this play in 1969. I am indebted to Malini, my daughter, for writing the earlier drafts, and to Jacqueline, my daughter-in-law, who spent many hours co-ordinating, revising and typing the final version of the manuscript. I would like to express my gratitude to Professor Ram Chandra Prasad, my preceptor and mentor, who has inspired and encouraged me for the last ten years and wrote the Foreword to this play. Finally, my heart-felt appreciation goes to my wife, Gomathi Tulsiram, who listened to the play at every stage. She was the sounding board to test the dramatic effect of the play. Without her love, encouragement and patience this book would not have been possible.

Ottawa, Canada NANDLAL TULSIRAM
November 1991

FOREWORD

Krishna Hari, one of the most readable plays ever written on the themes of Kamsa's atrocities and the birth of Krishna, reveals the mastery the dramatist has of Indian mythological materials. His knowledge of Indian scriptures, especially of *Shrimad Bhagavatam,* is both extensive and deep, one of the most welcome fruits of which is the display, a dramatization of one of the most important episodes in what is one of the greatest of the Hindu Puranas. That the play is enormously stageable will be apparent to every reader.

Tulsiram, its author, is a familier name in Africa—it's a name associated with the production of more than a score of plays centring around diverse themes, mostly culled from Indian mythology and tradition. Report goes that every member of the audience has appreciated Tulsiram's plays, his dialogues, his technique and art of characterization, his naturalism and realism and his profound knowledge of the dramatic art. In so far as *Krishna Hari* is concerned, it is remarkable for its pithy dialogues and crisp, lively sentences decorously suited to the characters, matching their character and personality. As he has already produced and directed no less than twenty-four plays, Tulsiram knows the taste of his audiences as he also knows what the stage requirements indeed are. Therefore, there are no loose ends here; instead, we have a well-knit plot, skilfully engineered and possessed of a remarkable organic unity in the Aristotelian sense of the term. The author writes with a commendable ease bordering on spontaneity and consummate expertise. The book, I am sure, will be popular and readily welcome for its readability, interesting themes, and dramatic art. Those who are interested in getting a first-hand information about one of the most significant episodes of the *Shrimad Bhagavatam*, its symbolically charged meaning, and its spiritual significance, will find in this play a remarkable contribution, in fact, the only dramatic contribution ever made in English. Therefore, I would recommend it to all lovers of English drama.

R. C. Prasad
M.A. (*Pat.*), PH.D. (*Edin.*), D. LITT. (*Pat.*)
Professor of English
Patna University, Patna, India

CONTENTS

CHARACTERS

MAHARAJA UGRASENA, *King of Mathura*

MAHARAJA KAMSA, *Usurper and King of Mathura*

DEVAKI, *Kamsa's sister and wife of Vasudeva*

VASUDEVA, *Prince—Devaki's husband*

KRISHNA/BALARAMA, *Sons of Devaki and Vasudeva*

YASHODA, *Wife of Nand and foster mother of Krishna*

NAND, *Yadav Chief and foster father of Krishna*

NARAD MUNI, *Sage*

AKRURA, *Kamsa's minister and Krishna's devotee*

RADHA, *Village maiden of Vrindavan and playmate and lover of Krishna*

PUTANA/BAKASURA, *Rakshasas in the employ of Maharaja Kamsa*

JARASANDHA, *King of Magadh*

GOPIS, *Village maidens of Vrindavan*

GOPAS, *Cowherds of Vrindavan*

RUKMINI, *Princess*

LEELA/GOMATI, *Women of Mathura*

TRIVAKRA, *Malini, deformed devotee of Krishna*

OLD MAN/WRESTLERS, *In the employ of Maharaja Kamsa*

Kings, Princes, Princesses, Ministers, Guards, Soldiers and Footmen.

ACT
1

ACT 1 SCENE 1

Maharaja Kamsa's Palace—Mathura

[*Maharaja Kamsa, the king of Mathura, is seated on the throne. Devaki, his sister, and Vasudeva, her bridegroom, who have just been married are sitting on a throne to the left of Kamsa. Pradhan Mantri, the king's Chief Minister, stands on his right. Maharaja Ugrasena, king Kamsa's father, sits close to the bridal couple. Maharaja Jarasandha of Magadh sits on another throne. Princesses Damayanti and Priyadarshini sit next to each other. Prince Dharmendra from Salya and Prince Madanjit sit facing the princesses. Yadava princes, court ladies, gentlemen, the king's retinue, occupy the stage. Narad Muni, the old sage, muses quietly in a corner. The stage is set for a dance.*]

MAHARAJA KAMSA. Venerable sage, Narad Muni, pranaam!

NARAD MUNI. Narayan! Narayan!

MAHARAJA KAMSA. Maharaja Jarasandha, our noble king and friend, kings, princes and princesses, lords and ladies, and my humble countrymen, my father King Ugrasena and I welcome you to this very providential, very auspicious occasion. We welcome the Yadavas, we embrace Vasudeva, the chief of the Shooras. We welcome our guests from Vrajabhumi.

THE CROWD. Maharaja Kans ki jai! Maharaja Kans ki jai!

MAHARAJA KAMSA. Today is a marriage of the Andhakas and the Shooras. Today, we become one. My heart is overflowing with joy to see my sweet sister Devaki happily married to noble Vasudeva. May you live a hundred years! It's time for rejoicing. The festivities will last for fifteen days. Pradhan Mantri, where are the dancers?

PRADHAN MANTRI. Yes, Maharaj. Here they come, Madhumati and Chitralekha, the dancing beauties from Vrindavan.

[*Enter Madhumati and Chitralekha. They first bow to Narad Muni and then to Maharaja Kamsa.*]

MAHARAJA KAMSA. [*Smiling*] The Pradhan Mantri has good taste. These dancers look like apsaras from the heavens.

[*Chitralekha and Madhumati dance.*]

MAHARAJA JARASANDHA. Oh, wonderful! These dancers are simply exquisite. Why, Chitralekha dances like Urvashi, the dancer from Indralok.

PRINCE DHARMENDRA. And Madhumati is a veritable angel. I have never seen anyone so fleet-footed, agile and sinuous as Madhumati. She is like a lotus fluttered by the gentle breeze and quivers like the lonesome peacock among the trees.

PRINCESS DAMAYANTI. Splendid, my little poet, splendid! You always have an eye for beauty. I am sure you are already intoxicated with her charm and grace. Yes, she dances like the apsara Menaka to win the heart of the divine sage Vishwamitra.

PRINCESS PRIYADARSHINI. Most certainly sister! Even prince Madanjit seems to be dazed by these lotus-eaters.

I must admit my heart is all a-flutter by the rhythm and poise of these dancers. They have succeeded in what Menaka failed to do.

PRINCE MADANJIT. But ladies, isn't Madhumati an angel and Chitralekha a swan? Even the gods will swoon when they see their fawn-like faces and doe-like eyes. Yes, this is perfect bliss.

[*The dancers bow again. Gold and silver ornaments are given to the dancers by Maharaja Kamsa and other members of the royal family.*]

DEVAKI. [*Holding Vasudeva's hand*] Nath, how happy I am!

VASUDEVA. Yes, princess, it's like a dream come true.

DEVAKI. Oh, my Vasudeva, royal Shoorasena, it seems to me we met many aeons before. I think you were a great monarch then and I was a pretty infatuated jealous queen. Do you remember anything of the past?

[*Vasudeva looks vacantly ahead of him. He seems to be in a state of sorrow.*]

Oh, my dear Prince, why do you look so cheerless and forlorn?

VASUDEVA. My dear charming daughter of Devaka, my precious Devaki, I remember nothing. Please forgive me if my joys are not unbounded, for I have dark foreboding, terrible joy, wordless sorrow. I shouldn't be, but this new-found happiness seems too fragile, too insecure. I sense terrible tidings. My heart is like a restless wave, so please bear with me awhile, it will soon calm down.

DEVAKI. Look, my dear Vasudeva, here comes my royal brother, Maharaja Kamsa, with his cheerful retinue.

[*Devaki and Vasudeva smile*]

MAHARAJA KAMSA. Pradhan Mantri, the time for the departure of the bridal party draws nigh. Let our honoured guests know the royal trousseau we have for the distinguished couple. Announce the dowry offered by the Bhoja dynasty to our beloved sister and brother-in-law.

PRADHAN MANTRI. Very well, Maharaj. Here is a short list of the main gifts we have for Prince Vasudeva and Princess Devaki:

Four hundred elephants, in stately attire, decorated with golden garlands, fifteen thousand bejewelled horses with stirrups made of diamonds and pearls, one hundred and eight chariots studded with rubies and precious gems—

THE CROWD. Maharaja Kans ki jai! Maharaja Kans ki jai!

PRINCESS DAMAYANTI. Silence, Princess Priyadarshini, it's not over yet.

PRADHAN MANTRI. [*Continuing*] For each chariot, a charioteer, two hundred beautiful damsels, and two hundred handsome men to accompany the bridal couple, golden plates and cups, priceless ornaments, great paintings, and clothes made of silks, satins and precious gems for every member of the bridal party.

THE CROWD. Maharaja Kans ki jai! Maharaja Kans ki jai! Maharaja Ugrasen ki jai! Maharaja Ugrasen ki jai!

MAHARAJA KAMSA. Pradhan Mantri, get my royal chariot, Madhur Sulochana.

PRADHAN MANTRI. Here comes Madhur Sulochana with four milkwhite horses.

[*The sound of chariot wheels*]

MAHARAJA KAMSA. My heart is like a bird and I feel an inner joy. I am in flightful ecstasy. I shall be the charioteer and will drive Madhur Sulochana to Vraj. My passengers will be my sweet sister Devaki and my dear brother-in-law Vasudeva. Come Devaki, come Vasudeva, let us go.

[*Maharaja Kamsa holds them by the hand and walks towards the chariot*.]

AKASH VANI. [*Music—sounds of distant drums*; *lightning and thunder*] Hear, Oh hear, Maharaja Kamsa, I am Akash Vani, the Voice of the Lord. The sister whom you have so happily given in marriage to Vasudeva will be your doom for her eighth-born son will be your *kaal,* your death! Your evil days are over. Beware! Beware!

[*Music fades—sound of distant drums*]

MAHARAJA KAMSA. What is it I hear? My sister's son to be my murderer? Munivar, enlighten me.

NARAD MUNI. Narayan! Narayan! What the God's will no man can put asunder. Infinite and mysterious are the ways of the supreme spirit.

MAHARAJA KAMSA. Devaki's son to be *kaal,* my death? Is it a demoniac trick to belittle the great Kamsa. No! No! This can never be. Oh, great sage, can this be true?

NARAD MUNI. [*Narad smiles derisively*] So does the Akash Vani say. Those who deny the laws of divine justice, those who reject dharma, must pay the penalty for their crimes. Divine law is immutable, unalterable, and no one can ever escape it. Narayan! Narayan!

MAHARAJA KAMSA. Devaki, did you hear that? Your son will be my murderer!

[*Holding her plaited hair*]

DEVAKI. My brother, Bhaiya, that cannot be!

KAMSA. [*Laughing hysterically*] Who can kill me? I am *kaal*, I am the death of Death. Even Yama, the God of Death, cannot kill me. Devaki, you must die!

DEVAKI. No Bhaiya, no! I am your sister, your treasure. Did you not pledge to my mother on her dying bed that you will care for me?

VASUDEVA. My lord, my king!

[*Kamsa pushes Vasudeva down.*]

KAMSA. Down, you miserable serpent! So have I nurtured and nourished a little viper in my royal household? Devaki, say your prayers!

VASUDEVA. Oh, Maharaja! Great father, have mercy!

KAMSA. Down, you wretch! You, too, shall die before you open your venomous jaws. Once I have killed you two what have I to fear? Devaki, have you said your prayers?

DEVAKI. Bhaiya! Bhaiya!

VASUDEVA. Oh great king, most noble sire, the glory of the Bhoja dynasty, spare your sister's life. You are her guardian, her elder brother, her king.

MAHARAJA UGRASENA. My son, let Devaki go. She is your sister. To kill a sister is a serious transgression. It is against dharma. Neither man nor God will forgive you.

KAMSA. Father, did you not hear the Akash Vani say that Devaki's eighth child will be the cause of my death? It is a timely warning: the gods have warned me and I will not let Devaki's offspring be the cause of my death.

MAHARAJA UGRASENA. My son, how long will you continue committing such shameful deeds? You have lost touch with your father, the rightful king, your subjects, and your country. You have already usurped my throne, had me imprisoned, incarcerated my royal subjects and killed thousands of innocent people. Have pity, my son! Spare Devaki's life. Let her go!

KAMSA. I took over your kingdom because you were a weak and foolish king. The prison is the safest abode for you. Guards, put this wretch back in prison.

VASUDEVA. Maharaja, noble sire, I beseech you to spare Devaki's life. Have no fear of your sister. The prophecy did not say that Devaki will kill you. Do not commit a terrible crime by killing your sister. Devaki and I promise you that we shall lay all our newborn babes at your feet, and you may do as you will.

KAMSA. [*Meditatively*] What if you break your promise?

VASUDEVA. Promises are not made to be broken, my lord.

DEVAKI. At your feet, my lord, shall we lay our newborn babes.

KAMSA. Be it so! But I must take every precaution to protect myself from the instruments of my death. Guards, take Vasudeva and Devaki to the east end of the palace prison. Let it be strongly fortified, guard them day and night.

[*All leave, but Narad Muni*]

NARAD MUNI. Narayan! Narayan!

Maharaja Kamsa thinks he is immortal, all tyrants think they will live forever. These merciless brutes, who are inspired by lust and greed, plunder, ravage, kill and destroy at will. Other demoniac kings share the spoils and continue to perpetuate evil. But God's hand is at work and His will shall be done.

Narayan! Narayan!

[*Exit Narad Muni.*]

END OF ACT 1 SCENE 1

ACT 1 SCENE 2

At the Foot of the Himalayas

VOICES. [*It is a stormy night and sages and saints chant the name of the lord.*] Ram! Ram! Ram! Ram!

[*Continuous chanting*]

THE HILL MAN. [*An old Hill Man on his crutches peers outside.*] Rajani! Ho Rajani! Rajani! What can this girl be doing with herself on a night like this. Rajani!

[*Shakes his head.*]

I am sure she has gone to see the Sadhus. Oh! It is too cold for a man like me. I must go back.

RAJANI. [*Loud footsteps can be heard. Rajani enters panting and very excited.*] Baba! Ho Baba! Ho Baba!

THE HILL MAN. [*Comes out of the hut*] What is it, my child?

RAJANI. Another Sadhu, Baba. Another holy man! He carries something in his hand and it makes music. Baba, why do they all come? There are over a hundred of them all along the mountain side.

THE HILL MAN. Oh, my dear daughter, you don't understand.

RAJANI. Some of them are young, some are old. Some of them have beards and only their two white eyes can be seen. Oh really, I don't understand. Some of them are clean-shaven and have no hair on their heads. My God, it is a wonder!

THE HILL MAN. Beti, you shouldn't be going out on a night like this. Come into the hut.

RAJANI. Some chant the name of the Lord. Some say "Ram! Ram!", some say "Jai Hanuman" and some say "Shiva! Shiva! Shiva!"

THE HILL MAN. Oh, Rajani, get into the hut. It is a bitterly cold night.

RAJANI. Baba look at him. [*Pointing to a sage*] He has been there for three months. He continues chanting "Ram! Ram!" All he has is a *lota* of water. There is one near the sacred Janak Talao of the Ganga. He has been sitting there for a year. An anthill has grown all around him. Ants move all over his body but he sits calmly meditating on the Lord.

THE HILL MAN. [*Lightning and thunder*] We expect more rain, Beti. Let us go in.

RAJANI. But Baba, they defy the weather—thunder, lightning, rain and snow. There was one who was sitting close to Mother's cremation ghat. A snake was entwined all around his neck but he continued saying "Ram! Ram !".

[*Footsteps can be heard.*]

THE HILL MAN. [*Holds Rajani's hand and leads her into the hut.*] Let us go in.

[*Enter Narad Muni and another sage.*]

NARAD MUNI. Narayan! Narayan!

SAGE. Namaskar Devarshi, Namaskar! What news do you bring?

NARAD MUNI. Evil continues at an alarming rate all over our beloved country. Each day a number of men and women are killed by the rakshasas. Maharaja Kamsa rules with an iron hand. His father Maharaja Ugrasena has been imprisoned with Devaki and Vasudeva.

SAGE. What is the news of Devaki and Vasudeva?

NARAD MUNI. Maharaja Kamsa has already killed six of their children and Devaki and Vasudeva continue their sad lives in prison. Fortunately, the seventh-born was still-born.

[*With a mischievous smile*] So they say!

SAGE. What is the news in Mathura?

NARAD MUNI. There is deep sadness in the hearts of the people. The Andhakas and the Shooras are an oppressed race. Maharaja Kamsa brooks no intervention. He has burned down the temples, trod upon the Brahmans and killed the sages. No one is safe in Mathura.

SAGE. Om Hari Om! There must be an incarnation of God soon. The load of sin is too heavy. Not even Mount Himalaya or the Ganga can bear the weight.

NARAD MUNI. Swamiji, let us pray. Oh Krishna Hari, wherever Thou art, come to us in our distress. Thy pilgrims need Thee, they call for Thee in this hour of need.

[*Rajani and The Hill Man leave their hut.*]

RAJANI. Let us speak to him, Baba.

THE HILL MAN. No, my child. Leave them alone.

[*Rajani darts out and prostrates on Narad Muni's feet.*]

NARAD MUNI. Narayan! Narayan! God bless you, my child.

RAJANI. Why are all these sages and saints praying around the Himalayas and Ganga?

NARAD MUNI. They are praying for the incarnation of God and they hope He will come down soon. They are waiting for an avatar.

RAJANI. Will the Lord come?

NARAD MUNI. Yada yada hi dharmasya
Glanir bhavati bharata
Abhyutthanam adharmasya
Tadatmanam srijamy aham.

Yes, my child. The Lord said that whenever and wherever there is a decline in righteousness and a rise of adharma or evil, my Spirit will arise on earth.

RAJANI. What will the Lord do on earth?

NARAD MUNI. Paritranaya sadhunam
Vinasaya ca duskritam
Dharma samsthapanarthaya
Sambhavami yuge yuge.

The Lord said that He will be born for the salvation of the good and the righteous and the destruction of evil.

He says that He will appear again and again, millennium after millennium. That is why, my child, the sages and saints are praying at the foot of the Himalayas and on the banks of the Ganga.

RAJANI. Swamiji, will He be born here? Will he come this way?

NARAD MUNI. [*Smiling*] No! No, my child, He will not be born here, but He will certainly come this way. He will be born in a prison.

RAJANI. In a prison, my Lord?

NARAD MUNI. Yes, my child, in a prison. The ways of the Lord are infinite.

Aparam paar prabhoo ki maya

Narayan! Narayan!

[*They all kneel down to pray.*]

END OF ACT 1 SCENE 2

ACT 1 SCENE 3

Prison in Mathura

VASUDEVA. [*Thunder, lightning and rain*] Devaki, can you hear the thunder rolling? It has been going on like this for two hours. Putana, our evil bodyguard has not returned yet. The only lights flickering are the ones in our dreary cell. But this must be a good omen. There are no sounds coming from the Magadhan guards. There is a peaceful silence in the raging storm. I think Devi.

DEVAKI. [*Holding Vasudeva's hand*] Nath, I think our saviour is coming.

VASUDEVA. [*Falls on the ground and begins to pray*] Om, Hari Om, Tat Sat.

Come, my Lord, we need Thee. We have waited long for Thy divine presence. Please come, my Lord.

DEVAKI. [*Touching his head*] Nath, He has come.

VASUDEVA. [*Looks up; sees Krishna in His divine glory. In His hands, He carries the discus, the mace, the conch and the lotus*] My Lord, my Krishna.

DEVAKI. My Prince, my Saviour, my Lord.

[*Krishna smiles, becomes a baby, and begins to cry.*]

(*Devaki and Vasudeva hold each other's hand and look in amazement at the baby crying on the floor.*)

DEVAKI. Nath, look at our baby.

VASUDEVA. To think we have to part with this little rosebud. Very soon the tyrant will be here. But where are the guards? They must have heard the baby crying.

DEVAKI. [*Fondling the baby*] Must this one go, too, Nath?

VASUDEVA. Your brother, Maharaja Kamsa, wills it so.

DEVAKI. My brother? What brother? I have no brother! He is a beast, an evil demon. Even a wild animal would have had more pity on me and my babes.

VASUDEVA. This is our karma, this is what we have to pay for our last sins. Oh God, have mercy on us!

DEVAKI. Must this one, my sweet little babe die? My son, my child, my little flower! Very soon this little lamp of light shall flicker no more and our last glimmer of hope will be lost forever.

VASUDEVA. Yes, Devi, and we shall be left in the dark again.

DEVAKI. Oh, Nath, why did we ever make such a fateful promise to the devil? We have already lost six of our children. Must this one, this little one, get into the hands of that monster?

VASUDEVA. How can we save him?

DEVAKI. No! No! No! This blossom must not be allowed to wither. [*Cries*] Oh little love-bird, will you not flit and twitter any more? Nath, look at this little moonbeam. Look at his silvery eyes and his petal-like lips. Ah, his cheeks are little lotus blossoms. Poor bird, must thou go?

[*Weeps*]

VASUDEVA. Patience, Devi, patience!

DEVAKI. Patience, my Lord, patience, did you say?

VASUDEVA. Yes Devi, but how can we save this child from the clutches of that monster?

DEVAKI. What a mother have I been?

VASUDEVA. And what a coward was I to see the rakshasas kill all our little babes! Look at those walls, they are smeared with our children's blood.

DEVAKI. My God, all my children, one by one, mercilessly killed. My heart was throbbing for their love and each time I was about to feed them, they were snatched away from my breast.

VASUDEVA. And I, Devi, stood and watched the sad spectacle. Even the birds will defend their young ones to the last.

AKASH VANI. [*The sound of music and drums*] Take the baby to Gokula, to Nand and Yashoda's abode. Replace him with the baby that has just been born to Yashoda.

DEVAKI. Nath, did you hear that voice?

VASUDEVA. No Devi, I didn't.

DEVAKI. Nath, take the baby to Gokula.

VASUDEVA. To Gokula?

DEVAKI. Yes, to Gokula, to the house of Nand and Yashoda.

VASUDEVA. But how can I, Devi? My feet are bound in chains. How can I set myself free?

[*The chains fall off.*]

DEVAKI. Go, Nath, go. Have faith in Him. He who guides the blind, sustains the crippled, will certainly guide you.

VASUDEVA. But all around us are Kamsa's rakshasas and the Magadhan guards. And the doors are barred.

[*The doors open and the guards are asleep.*]

DEVAKI. God is on our side, Nath. Look, all the guards are asleep! Go, Nath, go!

VASUDEVA. Oh, how my feet tremble! How will I be able to take him across the turbulent Yamuna?

DEVAKI. Go, Nath, go.

[*Places the child on a pannier.*]

Have faith in Him, He shall certainly take you across the Yamuna.

VASUDEVA. My son! My son!

[*Places the pannier on his head.*]

DEVAKI. My Krishna! My son!

[*Vasudeva leaves with the baby; kneels down in prayer.*]

Oh, Shankar-Parvati, the creator of the world, Oh, Mother Yamuna, take my Nath and my Baby safely to Gokula.

END OF ACT 1 SCENE 3

ACT 1 SCENE 4

Prison in Mathura

[*Some time later.*]

DEVAKI. How lonely I feel, my beloved Vasudeva has gone, and I am alone, alone, all alone, in this dark and gloomy cell! I wonder how my Nath crossed the Yamuna. Oh, God, I hope he is safe!

[*Sound of footsteps—Vasudeva enters.*]

Nath, Oh Nath! Nath! Nath, Nath!

VASUDEVA. Yes Devi, the gods came to my assistance.

DEVAKI. But have you come back with our baby?

VASUDEVA. No, Devi, I have left our precious jewel with Nand and Yashoda. When I got to Nandgaon everyone was asleep—Nand, Yashoda, servants, nurses, all asleep.

DEVAKI. And then?

VASUDEVA. Even the cows and the cowherds were asleep. Not a soul was stirring and that Nandgaon pasture seemed like heaven.

DEVAKI. And the baby?

VASUDEVA. Yashoda lay blissfully asleep and Nand was lying

snugly in a corner but this little girl at Yashoda's side lay wide awake and she looked at me beseechingly as if beckoning me to pick her up. I placed our son close to Yashoda and took this pretty little girl with me.

DEVAKI. Thank God! So our little son is saved! God has spared a child of mine and he may live to soothe our pain one day.

VASUDEVA. Our karma, Devi, our karma. We must have done some good deed to get such great assistance.

DEVAKI. How did you cross the Yamuna?

VASUDEVA. The Yamuna was in flood but I waded safely across Chitra's pool. No sooner did I enter the river than the water snakes and the water rose had touched my neck. I thought I was going to drown. But a miracle happened, the Little One lowered his feet to becalm the water and the water snakes. As soon as He had done that, the water subsided and sank so low that I was able to cross safely.

DEVAKI. Praise the Lord for delivering our son. But must this little angel die at the hands of my cruel brother?

VASUDEVA. Oh, Devi, I am sure the rakshasas won't kill this little girl. He may save her because she is a girl. And the prophetic words he heard may seem false to him.

DEVAKI. No, my brother won't spare this precious jewel. And our hearts will continue to bleed. Nath, look at this baby! She must be an angel, an apsara, who has come to our assistance. Only an angel will look so divine. Her eyes are like two stars shining in the lake, her cheeks are fresh as the morning dew and her lips are the colour of a crimson rose.

[*The baby cries—footsteps can be heard*; *Devaki and Vasudeva fasten the shackles on their feet and hands.*]

MAHARAJA KAMSA. Devaki, where is my *kaal*, my death?

DEVAKI. [*Holding the baby close to her bosom*] Please, Bhaiya, my dear brother, the baby is only a little girl. The omen said that my eighth-born child will be a son. The prophecy is wrong. She is your niece, please spare her.

MAHARAJA KAMSA. [*Trying to pull the child out of Devaki's hands*] Bring the little murderer here.

DEVAKI. No, Maharaj, she is a girl. Do not kill her. You have already killed six of my children. Do not add more sins on your soul. Spare her, my Lord!

MAHARAJA KAMSA. Her offsprings will do me harm, the prophecy willed it. Bring her here.

[*Struggles with Devaki but she passes the baby on to Vasudeva*]

VASUDEVA. Rajan, great Prince, my Lord, you will earn no honours by killing this poor innocent, defenceless little girl. Let her go.

[*Kamsa grasps the baby and looks tauntingly at her.*]

MAHARAJA KAMSA. So you are my *kaal*, my Death!

[*Laughs menacingly*]

Have you come to kill the mighty Kamsa? Let's see who can save you.

[*Tries to dash the baby on the prison walls. He raises his hands—but the baby flies away.*]

THE BABY—AKASH VANI. [*Sound of lightning and thunder; drums can be heard in the distance.*] Oh, Kansraj! What was the point in your trying to kill me. Your enemy has already been born and your death is near. Beware! Beware!

MAHARAJA KAMSA. What, cheated again! Rakshasas, go and kill every newborn babe in Mathura, let none live! Pralamba, get Pradyota and Putana to send as many of my faithful followers as possible. Go all over Mathura, and even beyond, if necessary.

END OF ACT 1 SCENE 4

ACT
2

Rathin

ACT 2 SCENE 1

Nand and Yashoda's Abode—Gokula

NAND. Yashoda, our world has changed considerably since this little darling came into our lives. There's an aura of freshness and beauty all around.

YASHODA. Yes, my Lord, it is like perpetual spring. Even the birds sing sweeter and longer. Krishna has illuminated our hearts and has filled this house with love and laughter.

NAND. What did sister Kamala say?

YASHODA. [*Laughing*] Oh, she does say funny things! She says Krishna looks like a little god.

NAND. A little god! Yes, Yashoda Devi, sometimes I think so too. The other day when he was playing under the peepal tree I heard someone laugh! Then I heard voices, and then there was that sweet thrilling laughter again. It was like a voice from the heavens. When he saw me he smiled, and then began to cry. He had become a baby again. He has an hypnotic charm which I cannot fathom. He must be a little god!

YASHODA. [*Smiles*] You are in love with your child, and your eyes and ears play tricks on you. It's strange, though, how his cheeks seem to change everyday. Sometimes, they are like living roses, sometimes they are pale like the waning moon. His eyes changed from childish playfulness to mature seriousness. Now and again I feel as if Krishna raises his eyebrow and laughs at me.

NAND. [*Laughing*] Does he say "foolish woman"?

YASHODA. Oh, no, no! He says, "Sweet Mother, I love you."

[*Enter two Gopis*]

Namaste, Shalini Devi.

SHALINI. Namaste, Yashoda Didi, meet my cousin Rekha Rani from Vrindavan.

REKHA. Namaste, Yashoda Didi.

YASHODA. Namaste, Rekha Rani. You are welcome to Gokula.

SHALINI. [*Smiling*] I was telling my cousin Rekha all about Krishna. He is Gokula's mascot and the gopis' darling.

REKHA. Isn't he a sweet a little fellow?

SHALINI. Yes, Rekha Rani. His face seems to tell me tales. He must have been my son in the last generation. See, how cosily he snugs into my arms.

YASHODA. Sister Rekha, what news do you bring from Vrindavan?

REKHA. Vrindavan is a virtual paradise. It's a haven for peace and quiet. But disquieting news comes from Mathura.

YASHODA. From Mathura?

REKHA. Maharaja Kamsa has ordered his rakshasas to kill every newborn babe born in Shravan. Mothers hide their babies from these monsters and are constantly alert. Two days ago two boys were taken from one village and killed.

YASHODA. Oh, my god, what an evil king!

REKHA. The children are always guarded jealously. Nine boys have already been killed. Many families with children are terrified of Kamsa's henchmen. Some of them are leaving Mathura surreptitiously. One family lives in hiding in Vrindavan. Anyone born in the month of Shravan is in danger.

SHALINI. The beast! Would the king send his spies here, too?

REKHA. Yes, they may even come here. The terrorists are in search of unusual babies, particularly boys born in Shravan. Be careful of Krishna, do not ever leave him alone.

YASHODA. Sister Rekha, our baby is never left alone. Two persons are always with him. He passes from one hand to another. He is Gokula's child and everyone in Gokula is responsible for him. But we will continue to take extra precautions.

[*Enter Atika Didi with a very pretty woman*]

ATIKA DIDI. Namaste Yashoda Bahen, meet Sushila Rani, the spouse of Bikash Tiwari from Roshan Gaon. All of us met her at the Mahadeva Mela along the Yamuna. We urged her to see our little Krishna before she left Gokula.

YASHODA. Welcome, Sister Sushila Rani, welcome! You have blessed our house with your presence. Thank you, Didi, for bringing such a charming person to our humble abode.

PUTANA. [*Disguised as Sushila Rani*] Thank you, Sister Yashoda, for your warm and cheerful welcome. I have heard so much about Krishna in the last two days that I decided to find some time to see him. Wherever and whenever I meet the good people of Gokula, their chief topic is about your darling little Krishna. Where is he?

SHALINI. Here, Sushila Rani, Krishna is all yours. We leave our dear Nand Lal to you.

YASHODA. Yes, sister, you are welcome to fondle our child. He is not only our child but he is the child of Gokula.

PUTANA. Oh, little one, your eyes are full of magic. I am sure you are going to break the hearts of many maidens.

YASHODA. Oh, sister, I am so glad you love my little one. Everyone does.

REKHA. Doesn't he look like a baby swan? Sister Sushila, what a beautiful picture you two make! The way the little greets, caresses you it seems as if he has known you for ages.

SHALINI. Come, Rekha Rani, let us go. My husband keeps telling me, "Shalini, the way you fondle and adore Krishna it seems to me you are reserving him as a partner for our little baby daughter".

[*Laughter; exit Shalini and Rekha.*]

YASHODA. Didi, will you walk with me to the orchard? I want to pluck a ripe mango for Krishna.

ATIKA. Sister Sushila, you can have the little darling all to yourself.

PUTANA. [*Disguised as Sushila Rani*] Come Krishna.

[*Laughs sardonically*]

Mother's darling, father's pride, gopis' playmate and Maharaja Kamsa's arch enemy. So you are going to be the husband of the gopis' unborn daughters? [*Smiles*] Come, Krishna, come! Taste boowa's milk. See if you can change the poison to honey. Poor dear, have your last suck!

[*Screams*]

Ah! Ah! Yashoda, Oh Yashoda. This is not a baby, he is my enemy, my murderer, my death! Help, help! He's killing me, he's sucking my life away. Oh! Ah! My life! Oh! Ah! Krishna! Krishna!

[*Falls to the ground; enter Atika, Yashoda, Nand, Gopis and Cowherds*]

ATIKA. Oh, God. She is Putana, the evil demoness.

YASHODA. My Krishna! My Krishna!

NAND. She is Putana, sent by Maharaja Kamsa to kill Krishna. Thank God he is safe.

YASHODA. My son! My son!

ATIKA. [*Kneeling in prayer*] Thank you Lord for saving our Krishna Kanhaya! Krishna! Krishna!

NAND. Maharaja Kamsa is at work. Thank God our little child is saved.

YASHODA. My son! Krishna! My lal!

[*Embracing Krishna and crying*]

NAND. Call the village brahman. Let's purify the house.

ATIKA. Krishna! Krishna!

GOPIS. Krishna! Krishna!

YASHODA. My Krishna! My son! My Krishna!

END OF ACT 2 SCENE 1

ACT 2 SCENE 2

Nand and Yashoda's Abode—Gokula

[*This is a room in Nand and Yashoda's house. Pictures of Shankar-Parvati, and Ram-Sita, and Hanuman are placed in the centre of the room. A camphor illuminates the* thali. *Two* thalis *of fruit serve as prasad. The village pandit has just completed the purificatory ceremony.*]

Yashoda passes the prasad around.

KRISHNA. Mother, may I now leave the room for a while.

YASHODA. Yes, my dear Krishna. Sisters Shalini and Rekha will accompany you.

VILLAGE PANDIT. Now that Putana is dead, Maharaja Kamsa will send other demons to kill Krishna. Be very careful of Kanhaya.

NAND. Yes, Panditji, we shall not keep him out of our sight. The two gopis are very reliable. At the gate we have two strong cowherds who will always keep an eye on our dear little one.

YASHODA. Maharaj, we are happy that Putana, the evil monster, is dead. Panditji, the good people of Gokula were overwhelmed by the aroma after Putana's cremation. Why was the air filled with the divinely perfumed smell?

VILLAGE PANDIT. I wonder! I wonder! I think our little Krishna must be divine. By allowing Krishna to suck her breast Putana attained salvation and by some divinely mysterious way the poison was transformed into a nectar of the gods. But, I must leave now. God be with you!

NAND. Yashoda, I'll take Panditji to the temple.

YASHODA. Namaskar Panditji. Thank you for your gracious help.

[*The village Pandit and Nand leave.*]

SHALINI. [*Enters the room in haste*] Yashoda bahen! Yashoda bahen!

YASHODA. Is Krishna all right?

SHALINI. Yashoda bahen, Krishna is eating sand.

[*Rekha holds Krishna by the hand and brings him into the room*]

REKHA. Look at his face, Yashoda bahen. It is covered with sand.

[*Krishna wipes the sand so quickly from his mouth that Yashoda was unable to see it.*]

YASHODA. Thank you sisters. Please leave Krishna with me and I shall deal with him.

[*Exit Shalini and Rekha.*]

Krishna, why did you eat sand?

KRISHNA. Me, mother? Why should I eat sand? Worms, mother, eat sand. Who says I ate sand?

YASHODA. [*Begins to sob softly*] Krishna, you tire me. Sisters Shalini and Rekha saw you eating sand. Even your brother Balarama saw you eat it.

KRISHNA. Mother, does a human being eat sand? Sand is not *laddoo* or *makkhan*. Why should I eat sand when you give me such tasty sweetmeats?

[*Laughs*]

YASHODA. [*Still sobbing*] Krishna! Krishna!

KRISHNA. My dear, dear mother, don't cry. Please don't cry! You can look into my mouth and see if I have eaten any sand.

YASHODA. Open your mouth Krishna.

[*Krishna opens his mouth. Mother Yashoda is stunned as she gazes at Krishna's mouth. She looks at him for some time without saying anything. She's hypnotized. There's a flash of light.*]

YASHODA. [*Holds Krishna towards her, sings him a lullaby, and puts him to sleep.*] Am I dreaming? Was that really a cosmic vision? Maybe, I have gone a little mad, a little insane!

[*Sobs softly. Nand enters the room and sees Yashoda crying.*]

NAND. Yashoda, what's the matter? Why are you crying? Has Krishna been up to mischief again?

YASHODA. No, my dear, no! Sisters Shalini and Rekha saw Krishna eating sand.

NAND. Eating sand? Why worry needlessly about that? Many children eat sand. That shouldn't make you cry.

YASHODA. When I asked Krishna to open his mouth I was astounded by what I saw. I was simply overwhelmed. I don't know whether it was real or a dream!

NAND. What did you see, Devi?

YASHODA. When his mouth was open wide I was simply entranced. A cool, soft and fragrant breeze engulfed me. I could hear the temple bells ringing. I felt a sense of exhilaration, a sense of eternal peace.

NAND. What did you see in Krishna's mouth?

YASHODA. I had a cosmic vision of the universal form of God. I saw the planets: the sun, moon, stars, all of them. I saw the entire elements ofthe universe: water, sky, earth and the heavens. I was simply amazed.

NAND. And then?

YASHODA. I rubbed my eyes to see if I was dreaming, but it was real. I saw mountains, lakes, rivers, oceans. I saw the birth of dawn, the shimmer off twilight. I saw the sunset fires. I saw you, I saw Gokula, I saw Vrindavan.

NAND. And then what did you do?

YASHODA. Then I heard the sound of kettledrums and the sweet musical sounds off the flute. The earth, the sky, the heavens and Gokula all seemed one.

NAND. And then my dear Yashoda Devi, what did you do?

YASHODA. I fell on Krishna's feet in silent benediction. I don't know how long I sat there. It was ecstasy, sheer divine ecstasy! When I opened my eyes Krishna began to cry. He became an infant again. I fed him, sang him a lullaby and put him to sleep. That can't be true, can it be my lord?

NAND. Mysterious are the ways of God. It must be true! It must be true!

YASHODA. Krishna! Krishna!

END OF ACT 2 SCENE 2

ACT 2 SCENE 3

Nand and Yashoda's Abode—The Courtyard: Gokula

YASHODA. Krishna, where's Balarama?

KRISHNA. He will be coming soon, mother. Mansook, the cowherd left me home. Bhaiya Balarama, Kashi and Sunil are still swimming in the Godavari pool. I become rather tired and hungry. Mother, do you have some curds and *dahi* for me?

YASHODA. Yes, my dear Krishna. I have curds, *dahi* and freshly made *rotis*. I know how you love *dahi* and *roti*.

KRISHNA. [*Eating ravenously*] Thank you, mother. They are very tasty. I seem to have such a good appetite this morning. Do you think I can have some more *dahi* and *roti*?

YASHODA. God bless you, my son. You are growing up beautifully. Your appetite is even better than your father's. That's good! Very soon you will become a cowherd and will have to take the cattle to pasture. Do you need any more curd?

KRISHNA. No, mother. You have already quenched my thirst and hunger.

[*Enter three gopis*]

ATIKA DIDI. Yashoda bahen, your son Krishna has been up to mischief again.

YASHODA. My son Krishna? What has he done now?

ATIKA DIDI. He and his friends have raided my house and emptied two pots of curd and *dahi*.

KAMALA. Yes, Yashoda Didi, Krishna, Balarama and three of his friends entered my house through the window. They ate everything and broke two pots.

YASHODA. But I have just fed Krishna. He was so hungry that he ate four *rotis* and three bowls of curd and *dahi*. Are you certain that my Krishna was the intruder and the thief? Krishna, is that true?

KRISHNA. No, mother, that's not true. I have spent the entire morning swimming at the Godavari pool.

YASHODA. That is what you said earlier.

[*With tears in her eyes*]

Kahn, did you really cause so much harm to Kamala bahen and Atika Didi?

KRISHNA. No, mother, no. Atika Didi's son Uddhava is a friend of mine. He loves milk, curds and butter. How do you know if he didn't steal the curd and *dahi*?

YASHODA. Krishna! Krishna!

[*In tears*]

KAMALA. My dear Yashoda Didi, we are sorry that we made you cry. But I caught the boys red-handed in my house. Kashi, Balarama, Sunil, Uddhava and a few others formed a three-tiered ladder. Balarama, Sunil, Kashi and Uddhava were at the bottom, three other boys were on top of them, and the last one was Krishna. Krishna had already made a hole in the curd pot and was busy eating. As soon as they saw me they dashed out wildly. Two pots fell and broke. They left me speechless. [*cries*] This is the third time that they have done it. I don't know how I am going to feed my husband and my mother-in-law.

YASHODA. Please forgive me Atika Didi and Kamala bahen. Kamala bahen, please take these two pots of curd and *dahi*.

[*Hands it to Kamala*]

I will punish Krishna severely.

[*Yashoda finds a stick to beat Krishna. As she approaches him Krishna begins to cry.*]

KRISHNA. Mother, I won't do it again. I promise you.

YASHODA. [*Yashoda throws the stick away. She ties Krishna with a rope to large mortar nearby.*] I will not let you go out of my sight. You will remain in this courtyard until your father returns.

ATIKA DIDI. Yashoda bahen, don't be too hard on Krishna. He has brought a lot of good luck and happiness to Gokula.

KAMALA. Yes, Yashoda bahen, Krishna is the mascot of Gokula. Since his birth the weather has been very good.

There has been neither flood nor famine since our Kahn came. Even the cows give more milk. Do treat him kindly!

YASHODA. Krishna, I am going into the house to do my daily chores. I know you will not be able to leave this place because I have tied you to a heavy mortar.

KRISHNA. [*Krishna looks around, smiles*] How long will I be tied to this stake? If I drag this mortar, my brother Balarama or my friend Sunil will set me free.

[*He tries to pull the mortar but he is unable to move even an inch.*]

No, I need some divine help to pull this heavy object.

[*He smiles. There's a flash of light and he moves with ease.*]

Oh, my path has been blocked by these two Arjuna trees. I think I'll go through them. It's so narrow I can't pass. I think I'll have to clear the path by breaking down the trees.

[*Smiles. There's a flash of light and the two trees fall with a thud. A man emerges from either side of the tree. Krishna is transformed into His divine glory; there is another flash of light.*]

NARAD MUNI. Narayan! Narayan!

[*Both men prostrate on the feet of Narad Muni*]

Sons of Kuvera, Nala and Mani, the curse is lifted. You have now come in the divine presence of the lord. Pay homage to the divine Krishna.

[*Both men prostrate on Krishna's feet*]

Nala and Mani, you have paid the penalty for your indiscretions. Remember to treat a woman with love and respect. A woman is a mother, a wife, a sister, a daughter! The divine Mothers are Lakshmi, Saraswati and Parvati. A man is not superior to a woman, they are equal partners. The progeny of the world depends on both sexes. Always remember that! By touching the feet of the Lord you have gained salvation from this life.

Narayan! Narayan!

[*Narad Muni and the two men leave quickly. Krishna begins to cry. Enter Radha and Shanta*]

SHANTA. Krishna, why are you crying? [*Looks around*] Krishna, who has tied you up to this mortar?

KRISHNA. My mother did. I behaved so badly that she fastened me to the mortar. She did not want me to leave the courtyard, but it is so distressing to lie so idle, almost as lifeless as this mortar. So I dragged the mortar through the trees.

RADHA. Poor Krishna! So you are Krishna, the son of Nand and Yashoda? What a heartless thing for a mother to tie up her own son. Come, let me unfasten you.

KRISHNA. Oh no, mother is very gentle and kind. She adores me. She gets angry sometimes and I love to see her anger subside. It's like the sun coming out on a rainy day. My mother is as warm and friendly as the sunshine in winter. Let her untie the knot.

RADHA. But my dear Krishna Kanhaya, there's mud and soot on your face. Shall I wash your face?

KRISHNA. Shanta, I do not think I can make your pretty cousin work. Will you please get me a jug of water from the Yamuna?

RADHA. Are you the little mischief-maker of this idyllic town?

KRISHNA. [*Smiling*] Mischief-maker?

RADHA. Yes, the gopis complain of you adoringly, they chastise you lovingly, they invite you to make mischief, Krishna, I remember meeting you many aeons ago.

[*Shanta enter with the water. Radha washes Krishna's face. Krishna smiles cheerfully.*]

KRISHNA. Yes, Radha, you are the mysterious girl I have met many ages ago. Are those dimples real?

RADHA. Oh, Krishna!

[*Enter Nand, Yashoda, gopis, cowherds and Balarama.*]

YASHODA. [*Rushing towards Krishna*] My son! My son! Forgive me for tying you up so long. My Kahn, did you pull out these two Arjuna trees?

KRISHNA. No, mother, the mortar did.

NAND. [*Embracing Krishna*] My son, thank god, you are safe. It's a miracle that these sturdy trees did not fall on you.

GOPIS. It's a miracle! A miracle!

KRISHNA. Mother, meet Radha from Vrindavan. She is nature's child, Yamuna's playmate, and the guardian of the cows.

RADHA. [*Prostrating on Yashoda's feet*] Mother, it's good to meet you.

YASHODA. Bless you, my child. I hope you will see us again. [*Radha prostrates at Nand's feet*] Greetings, my lord. I am very happy to meet my Kahn's father.

NAND. Bless you, my daughter. May you blossom and flourish! God be with you!

YASHODA. Krishna, my son, let us go into the house.

[*Moves in*]

KRISHNA. Radha, when shall I meet you again?

RADHA. At Vrindavan, along the banks of the Yamuna.

KRISHNA. At Vrindavan, at Vrindavan!

END OF ACT 2 SCENE 3

ACT 2 SCENE 4

Along the Banks of the Yamuna—Vrindavan

[*The sound of Krishna's flute fills the vale with music.*]

SAVITRI. Krishna's flute?

KAMINI. Yes, Savitri Devi, he fills the vale with music, love and laughter. Each time I hear that divine melody I swoon in ecstasy.

SAVITRI. Vrindavan, a haven of peace and beauty, has now become an abode of the gods. Listen! Can you hear the myriad sounds of this valley?

KAMINI. Yes, and everyone is in blissful accord! Yamuna, the sacred river, is eternally singing her lullaby, the trees sway their branches in perfect unison, the birds sing in rapture and our dear Krishna is the band leader.

SAVITRI. Since Chief Nand and Yashoda came to Vrindavan, there is an aura of cheerful homeliness. All of us have become one family.

[*There's a sound of silent sobbing*]

KAMINI. I wonder who can break the silence of this bejewelled grove by her silent sobbing.

[*Savitri and Kamini leave, Radha enters quietly wiping her tears.*]

RADHA. Krishna! Krishna! Why do you vex me so? My sad thirsty eyes are longing for you and my painful heart cries in agony for your love. Oh, why do you allow them to chase you like a deer? I am jealous of seeing the gopis in mad pursuit of you. I hate you, I hate you!

[*Music of Krishna's flute gets closer.*]

Oh, but that sound intoxicates me, it makes me mad!

[*Sits in a mournful pose*; *enter Mayna and Sarisha.*]

MAYNA. Who is this pretty maid moaning and pining along the banks of the Yamuna?

[*Radha raises her head.*]

Oh, Radha, what's breaking your heart?

RADHA. Leave me alone! I shall sit here and weep!

SARISHA. Till the Yamuna is in flood! [*Smiles*] Oh, Radha, it is spring and the valley is alive. Can you hear the mating call of the *koel*? Even the calves are frolicking like new-roused fawns.

RADHA. Don't talk to me about the *koel* or the *bulbul*. I have no ears to hear!

SARISHA. Because, my dear Radha, your amorous Kahnha goes after the wild ones and leaves you alone.

MAYNA. What does she say Sarisha?

SARISHA. Oh, don't ask me. She has fallen head over heels in love with Krishna.

MAYNA. Yes, look how she yearns and pines for him. But Krishna loves to tantalise the other gopis to make her jealous.

[*Enters Krishna*]

Look, here comes Krishna!

RADHA. I'll not speak to him.

[*Bows her head in silent sobs*.]

KRISHNA. Have anyone of you seen Radha?

SARISHA. She is down yonder, in the mango grove, pining for you.

[*Krishna walks to the mango grove.*]

RADHA. Krishna! Krishna!

MAYNA. Let us stay and hear the lovers' quarrel.

SARISHA. Oh, no! Let us go. It is spring, the month of lovers. Leave them alone.

[*The gopis go out laughing*.]

KRISHNA. Radha Rani, Queen of Vrindavan, where were you hiding?

RADHA. Under your favourite mango tree.

KRISHNA. Oh, no! You were not there, I have gone past the mango orchard several times.

RADHA. Leave me alone, I won't talk to you.

KRISHNA. Sweet Radha, pretty Radha, do look up!

RADHA. Leave me alone.

[*Head still bowed*]

KRISHNA. Well, then, I'll leave.

[*Makes a point of walking away*]

RADHA. Krishna, Oh Krishna, you do break my heart!

KRISHNA. Radha! Radha! Princess of the Grove, why are you so angry?

RADHA. Krishna Kanhaya, Murali Manohar, the flute-bearer of Vrindavan, will you ever understand my sorrowful plight? I have been waiting, and waiting, and waiting!

KRISHNA. Come, Radha. Let us walk along the crooked lane. This is an enchanted lane. See how the silvery moon plays softly on the Yamuna's breast and she sparkles with delight.

RADHA. Krishna, isn't it dangerous to walk alone on this crooked lane? I believe some evil demons secretly hide in the thick glade.

KRISHNA. Alone, alone, did you say? How can I ever be alone with you? Don't you know that Krishna is Radha and Radha is Krishna?

RADHA. You are mine and I am yours. My dear flute-player, sweet Giridhar, the sound of your music fills me with rapture and stirs memories of long, long ago. Have we ever met before?

KRISHNA. Yes, Radha, we have met from age to age. You represent the ideal but illusive lover, living in an idyllic paradise for whom men have longed for from time immemorial.

RADHA. And you my Krishna Hari, my Kahn, the pilot of my soul, will be remembered for all eternity. But we talk too much. Come, let us quench our thirst from the bubbling waters of the Yamuna so that our hearts melt and fuse into one.

KRISHNA. But we're two.

RADHA. Now, we two have become one, in the same way as the moonbeams have become wedded to the glittering Yamuna.

KRISHNA. Come Radha Rani, dance for me, and I shall play the flute.

RADHA. Yes, my Krishna. Radha will always dance for you. The nectar of your voice will never quench my thirst. Oh, my Murali Manohar, my eternal companion, play for me. Let the whole of Vrindavan rejoice at the sound of your music. Put your honeyed lips on the flute and let the magic of the sounds stir every living thing in this peaceful paradise.

[*Radha prostrates on Krishna's feet, he lifts her, and begins to play his flute*: *Radha dances. After the dance Krishna embraces her.*]

KRISHNA. The bowers of Vrindavan have become more radiant than Indralok and you, my dear Radha, are an apsara. You have become a legend: the ideal and idyllic, and millions of girls will be called Radha.

RADHA. And you, my Shyam Sundar, has made Vrindavan a shrine, a sanctuary. This place will be worshipped and revered for ages to come.

[*A loud thunder—and a monster in the shape of a large bird appears*.]

Look, Krishna, a demon! It looks like a giant bird.

KRISHNA. Yes, my Radha, it is a demon. Run, get under the peepal tree. The beast is Bakasura, a vicious demon, trained by Kamsa to kill his enemies.

RADHA. Be careful, Krishna. His body is as solid as a hill and his beaks look like two huge sharp swords.

BAKASURA. [*Laughing hysterically*] So you are Krishna! I wish Maharaja Kamsa had seen your frail and puny body. He would have crushed you in the palms of his hands. Beware Krishna, your death is near! No one ever escapes my razor-like beaks. I will cut you into a thousand pieces and feed you to the fish in the Yamuna. You will never escape my clutches. Not the whole of Vrindavan will be able to save you.

KRISHNA. Many evil demons have made the same threats. Do your worst. Come, let us fight.

[*They fight. Krishna holds both beaks and separates them. Bakasura lets out a roar of pain. Many people from Vrindavan come pouring in. Balarama, Kashi, Sunil, Uddhava and other gopikas come in.*]

BALARAMA. Krishna, are you safe?

KRISHNA. Yes, Bhaiya. Bakasura, the evil demon is no more and I am pleased that another evil monster is dead.

KASHI, SUNIL & UDDHAVA. Thank god! Jai Krishna Hari!

[*Enter gopis*]

MAYNA. Radha, are you all right?

RADHA. Yes, my dear, friends. If one has the sanctuary of Krishna there's nothing to fear. My Lord is Hari, Krishna Kanhaya, the indestructible.

GOPIS & GOPIKAS. Krishna Hari! Krishna Hari!

[*Plays his flute. More gopas and gopis come. They form a circle and dance the Garbha dance. Radha and Krishna occupy the centre stage.*]

END OF ACT 2 SCENE 4

ACT 2 SCENE 5

Nand and Yashoda's Abode—The Courtyard: Vrindavan

[*Seated in the courtyard are Nand, Yashoda and Akrura, the Chief of the Vrishnis.*]

NAND. My dear Akrurji, Yashoda, my family and I welcome Maharaja Kamsa's august representative to our humble abode.

YASHODA. Sire, the chief of the Vrishnis, you have brought the grace of the lord, to our house and family. Your saintly presence has sanctified Vrindavan, the cowherds, and their families. Welcome, my lord!

AKRURA. My dear Yashoda and Nandji, Vrindavan's effulgent glow has brought peace to my soul. This is the greatest pilgrimage I have ever made. I began my soul's journey from a state of ignorance but have now reached a state of perfect bliss. Divinity and grace rule this place. The Yamuna river, the trees, the shrubs, the birds, the cows, gopis and gopas, and the presence of your two divine sons clearly make this place an abode of the gods.

[*With tears in his eyes*]

Thank you for your warm welcome!

YASHODA. My dear Akrurji, we are overwhelmed by your

praise of our beautiful Vrindavan. We, too, love our pastoral abode. My dear lord, I do hope you bring good news from Mathura.

AKRURA. Maharaja Kamsa has just returned from a very successful mission. He is proud of his successes, happy that he followed the horse used in the Ashwamedha, the Horse Sacrifice. His father-in-law King Jarasandha of Magadh has showered him with imperial honours, gifts and large tracts of land. He has extended the Yadava domain and is celebrating his victory by having a royal party. I have come to invite you to the forthcoming activities.

NAND. To invite us to a royal party? The last festive occasion organized by Maharaja Kamsa was Devaki and Vasudeva's wedding which ended most tragically. I wonder if he wants to reassert his authority over the Yadava chiefs?

AKRURA. Maharaja Kamsa is in a joyous mood. He wants you and your two sons Krishna and Balarama to attend also.

YASHODA. Our sons Balarama and Krishna?

AKRURA. Yes, he wants them to participate in the bow sacrifice. The festivities will last for a week. There will be feats of military strength, wrestling, fencing, music, dancing and the Dhanuryajna, the bow sacrifice. Chief Nandji, he wants you to bring Balarama, Krishna and your annual tribute.

NAND. But, Akrurji, our sons are very young. Our Krishna is only sixteen years old. How will they be able to compete with Maharaja Kamsa's stalwarts?

YASHODA. Krishna and Rohini's son, Balarama, are dear and near to us as life itself. They are the life and light of this place and to part with them, even for a short time, will cast a gloom over Vrindavan. Reverend sire, my heart has already begun throbbing. I fear this invitation is fraught with something deep and sinister. Nandji, please don't send them.

AKRURA. Your two sons are glowing with transcendental light. Have faith in them. They are lion among men: strong, resolute of purpose, compassionate. They will change the course of destiny. Hasn't Krishna shown his extraordinary prowess by killing demons in Gokula and Vrindavan? Hasn't he vanquished Trinivarta, Bakasura and Dhenakasura? Let him go. The people of Mathura wait for him.

[*Enter Krishna and Balarama. They fall on Akrura's feet.*]

Arise Krishna! Arise Balarama!

[*With tears in his eyes and folded hands, as if in benediction, Akrura looks at Krishna for some time.*]

My lord, glory to Thee! Murali Manohar, Madhusudana, Krishna Kanhaya, my earthly pilgrimage is over.

[*Embraces Krishna*]

KRISHNA. Revered sire, I hope you bring glad tidings from Mathura.

AKRURA. Yes, I do. I bring you a personal invitation from His Royal Highness, Maharaja Kamsa to attend a grand mela, a fiesta, to celebrate his recent victories. You and your brother Balarama are invited. Maharaja Kamsa has sent his royal chariot to transport you to Mathura.

KRISHNA. That's good news indeed! I have been waiting patiently for a long time to visit Mathura.

BALARAMA. I have heard so much about the regal splendour of Mathura, the beautiful city across the Yamuna. And then to be the guests of Maharaja Kamsa in an honour indeed!

KRISHNA. Father, do we have your permission to leave?

NAND. Yes, Kahn, you do. You will leave early in the morning. You and Balarama will travel with sage Akrura. I will follow later. Balarama, inform your mother of our intentions and get her permission.

[*Balarama bows at Akrura's feet and leaves the courtyard; Yashoda cries.*]

KRISHNA. Why are you crying, mother? I shall be gone for only a week. Mother, you should be proud of your son for he has been invited to a royal command performance. Grant me leave to go with a cheerful heart. My brother Balarama and my dear father, the chief of Vrindavan, will accompany me. Give me your blessing!

AKRURA. My dear Krishna, I am sure you already know that you are not the son of Nand and Yashoda.

NAND. Not our son? What are you talking about Akrurji?

YASHODA. [*Laughing*] If not our son, then whose son is he?

AKRURA. He is the eighth son of Devaki and Vasudeva.

Listen, Krishna, you are a prince. You were born to redeem the suffering of the Yadu race and destroy wicked Kamsa.

KRISHNA. And Balarama?

AKRURA. He is the seventh son of Devaki and Vasudeva. I left him with Rohini at the dead of night.

YASHODA. My Kahn, my Krishna, my little flute-bearer is not my son?

KRISHNA. Yes, mother I am their son. So is Balarama. But you will always be my mother!

NAND. My son, you are a prince. Akrurji, does Maharaja Kamsa know?

AKRURA. Yes, he does.

NAND. Kamsa is an evil wretch. He will certainly want to kill Krishna. Kamsa is a blood-thirsty tyrant. He has already killed six of our children. Akrurji, pleases leave Krishna in Vrindavan.

YASHODA. Krishna, my love, you are the son of Vraj. Kamsa will kill you. Don't go my son!

AKRURA. Listen, my dear Yashodaji, Shri Krishna was born to rid the world of evil. The Akash Vani, the voice of the lord, sounded the divine message at Devaki and Vasudeva's wedding and Narad Muni, the Devarshi confirmed the proclamation. A special providence gave you, Nand and Yashodaji, a special privilege to nurture and nourish a great soul like Shri Krishna for sixteen years. You have done your duty. But now another chapter dawns in the life of Krishna.

KRISHNA. Mother, have no fear, I will come back to you.

NAND. No, my son, you will not come back. You are the son of Devaki and Vasudeva and they need you. You are a prince, my dear, and very soon will become the King of the Shooras. I always thought you were a God. The gopas and gopis thought so, too.

KRISHNA. Noble sage, what news do you bring of my mother and father?

AKRURA. Maharaja Kamsa is a cruel and a heartless king. He has treated your parents abominably. As soon as he knew that Devaki and Vasudeva were your parents he has incarcerated them again. Those two innocent human beings have become jail-birds. Your grandfather, king Ugrasena, the rightful king of Mathura, is in the same prison.

NAND. Go, my son, go! I will take Akrurji to our guest chamber. Please forgive me noble sire, for not paying attention to your needs!

AKRURA. My dear Nand and Yashodaji, tomorrow we leave at the rise of dawn. May I take your leave now?

YASHODA. God be with you!

AKRURA. Devaki Nandan, my dear son of Devaki, my charioteer and I will be waiting for you early in the morning.

[*Akrura and Nand leave.*]

YASHODA. Devaki Nandan! So you will no longer be Nand Lal, Brij Lal or Yashoda pootra? Devaki, I believe, keeps a doll to remind her of her son. You, my dear Krishna, will be ingrained in my heart and soul forever. Every moment, everyday, waking or sleeping, I shall think of you, my son. [*Cries*] I don't know how I can live without you.

KRISHNA. Don't cry, mother. I will think of you always. I shall never forget that I drank your milk, bore your love and caresses for sixteen years. You have been an ideal mother. How can I ever forget you? A thousand mothers with all their love will not be able to give me the love and devotion I got from you. My heart will always be with you mother, my father, and Vrindavan.

YASHODA. When again shall I be able to call you Murali Manohar, my Kanhaya, my Giridhari? When again will I be able to clasp your lotus feet? My son! My son!

[*Sobs*; *Radha enters and prostrates on Yashoda's feet.*]

Radha, what will you do without your Shyam Sundar, your dark handsome prince? Your Kanhaya will be gone forever. Stop him, if you can.

[*Embraces Radha. Krishna tell Radha everything. Yashoda gets back into the house.*]

KRISHNA. Have you heard the news?

RADHA. Yes, and Vrindavan is mourning your departure. There's a deep sadness in the hearts of everyone. Gopas and gopis are crying for you. My dear Kanhaya, how can I live without you? Please don't go!

KRISHNA. Have no fear, Radha, the absence will be short.

Once, I have done my duty I shall return to take you to Mathura. You will always be my soul's joy, my heart's delight, my lotus flower, the jewel of Vrindavan, I'll come back for you.

RADHA. My Kanhaya, how can I stop you from going to Mathura? You are a chosen one and providence has grand designs for you. Your mother and father need you, dharma ordains it. Kamsa will be vanquished, you will attain fame and glory. You are already a crown prince. Very soon you will become a great king. Go, my Krishna, go!

KRISHNA. And you, Radha, the crest-jewel of Vrindavan will be my queen. Your presence in the palace will add beauty to beauty. The garlands on your neck, my dear Radha Rani, will outshine the gems and precious pearls of royalty. Radha, you are beautiful, good and sublime! Be ready. I shall come for you to become my bosom companion, my joy, my love, my queen!

RADHA. No, my Giridhar Gopal, no! Remember, I am only a cowherd girl, Nature's child, lover of the bowers of Vrindavan. What would a cowherd girl know of royalty, palaces and court etiquette? Princesses will swoon over you and kings and queens will want you as a suitor for their daughters. You will become a great king and move about with royalty. And I will always remain an insignificant cowherd girl from Vrindavan. Go, my Kahn, go.

KRISHNA. Have we not occupied the centre of the stage in Vrindavan? Haven't you been my graceful dancing partner? Come, Radha, you would be the jewel of my crown!

RADHA. Krishna, didn't you say that I am an ideal but illusive lover, living in an idyllic paradise? My idyllic paradise is Vrindavan and my ideal love is a cowherd, a flute-player, dressed in blue and yellow. He has flowers in his ears and a peacock feather on his head. Krishna, you will always be here!

KRISHNA. But, Radha, won't you miss me?

RADHA. No, Krishna, you will be eternally in my thoughts. You will always be with me in Vrindavan. When mother Yamuna tosses and turns I'll hear your voice in her waves. Oh, charmer of hearts, Oh Kanhaya, Oh flute-bearer of Vrindavan, you will be ever present with me. When I hear the plaintive cry of the cuckoo my heart will swell with ecstasy. I'll rest under your favourite tree in the mango-orchard, the lover's nest, and I will once more hear your flute, your babble, your laughter. Go, my Krishna, go. You are a king.

KRISHNA. Yes, Radha, you are an apsara, a nymph, an epitome of eternal loveliness! You are a rare flower, a precious gem, that belongs exclusively to Vrindavan. I cannot take you away from it.

RADHA. Krishna, play your flute once more. I shall keep the sound of that melody for all eternity. Call the gopas and the gopis. Make it the last call, the final call!

[*Krishna plays the flute. Radha, with tears in her eyes, embraces Krishna*; *the gopas and gopis come flocking.*]

SUNIL. Oh Keshav, Oh prince among men, is this really the final call?

[*Sobs loudly*]

ATIKA DIDI. Murali Manohar, I'll fill my jars with the best curd and butter for you. Oh Krishna!

[*Cries*]

MAYNA. Oh, Damodhar, are you really leaving us?

[*Sobs silently*]

SHALINI. My Shyam Sundar, you won't forget us, will you?

UDDHAVA. My dear friend, my Keshav, my soul! Take me with you!

KASHI. Oh, God of the Shrine, will you leave us all alone?

[*Tears in his eyes*]

REKHA. Farewell, Krishna Kanhaya, flute-bearer of Vrindavan!

[*In loud sobs*]

RADHA. Krishna! Krishna!

END OF ACT 2 SCENE 5

ACT 3

Rathin

ACT 3 SCENE 1

Along the Banks of the Yamuna—Mathura

AKRURA. My dear Krishna and Balarama, this is Chitra's pool, a place of good omen. Prince Vasudeva's first test was to cross the stony ridge past Chitra's pool. It was a rainy and stormy night and the raging torrents completely covered the ledge, but the prince was able to take you safely across to Gokula.

KRISHNA. Good. Let us bathe and pay our homage to mother Yamuna. This will give father time to arrive in Mathura before we do. I am sorry I have missed the journey on the bullock cart. I am certain, the venerable bulls, Ram and Raja, will miss me.

BALARAMA. But I prefer the chariot, the monarch of the road, with its fleet-footed horses. The galloping horses give me a peculiar thrill. Let us stay here longer so that we can exercise the horses to the fullest.

KRISHNA. But we will tire the horses needlessly and we won't be able to admire and appreciate the beautiful landscape of Mathura. We have all the time in the world. Let us trot gently and gracefully to Mathura.

AKRURA. No, Krishna, time is running out. The whole world is waiting for your valorous and divine deeds. Your mother and father are longing to embrace you and

Balarama. The people of Gokula are restless and impatient of your delay.

KRISHNA. Yes, my revered sire, I agree. But they have already waited for sixteen years and a few hours won't make the difference. I think it will be wrong for me to get there before my mother and father. Mahatmaji, will you deny me the pleasure of admiring my Uncle's cherished and prized gardens?

[*Krishna and Balarama move towards the Yamuna.*]

AKRURA. [*Soliloquy*] Pardon me, Oh Gods, for my lack of faith! Does this handsome prince really possess divine power? Does he have the miraculous power to redeem mankind? Sometimes, I think he is far too handsome and likeable to perform heroic deeds. He is a charming flute-player, a friend of young men, and darling of the gopis of Vrindavan. Is he really the incarnation of the Lord who could free the Yadava race from Maharaja Kamsa's tyranny? Is he really the king of dharma? Forgive me, Oh Gods, but I must find out!

[*Walks towards Krishna. Prostrates on his feet.*]

KRISHNA. Arise, divine Akrura, arise! What is the need for this genuflection, this worship?

AKRURA. Forgive me, Krishna, but I need some assurance.

KRISHNA. What is it noble sire?

AKRURA. Do you know your mission in life? Do you know why you were born?

KRISHNA. [*Smiling*] Yes, to have two mothers and two

fathers! I have just bid farewell to one and will soon greet the other.

AKRURA. Do you know who you really are?

KRISHNA. Yes, I am the eighth son of Devaki and Vasudeva. I am to destroy uncle Kamsa and rid the world of evil. Is that not so, my dear Akrurji?

AKRURA. But my dear Krishna, Kamsa and his soldiers are invincible. The Magadhan guards patrol the palace. Your mother and father are scrupulously guarded. Kamsa wants to kill you before you accomplish the prophetic words of the *Akash Vani.* My heart is troubled. Please give me some assurance to alleviate these foolish misgivings.

BALARAMA. So our uncle Maharaja Kamsa has invited us to kill us? Is that so Akrurji?

AKRURA. Yes, that is so.

KRISHNA. [*Smiling*] Be of good cheer, Akrurji. Take your bath and complete your ablutions. Do not make the venerable Chitra wait for you.

BALARAMA. Yes, my dear Akrurji, what the gods will no man can put asunder. Krishna and I will vanquish the demons. Kamsa has scoffed the gods, mocked and jeered the sages, silenced the voice of reason, killed innocent babes. He is an arch enemy of dharma. His days are numbered.

Krishna, I am going to water and feed the horses. Akrurji, the cooling waters of the divine Yamuna await you.

AKRURA. [*With folded hands*] Please, my dear Lord, give me a sign, a sign like Hanuman gave Sita in Lanka. My good lord, a sign! A sign!

KRISHNA. Go my dear Akrurji, Yamuna will satisfy your curiosity and need.

[*Krishna goes towards the river.*]

AKRURA. [*Arms folded, Akrura looks beseechingly towards Krishna.*] Oh, Divine Father, Infinite Lord, your devotee longs for you.

[*Akrura looks at a beam of light. It is a halo just above the water. He gazes intently for some time. Then he falls on his feet.*]

Oh, Lord of the Universe, I bow down to Thee and seek Thy grace. Thy form is infinite.

[*Raises his hand in benediction—his eyes are full of tears.*]

Oh, monarch universal, Thou art manifest in every form. Thou art imperishable. Thou art the god of gods! I have seen Thy infinite majesty. I have seen the sun, the moon, the stars and the planets whirling around you. I now feel composed again in mind: I am myself again.

[*Krishna enters—and Akrura prostrates on his feet.*]

Oh, Krishna, I have seen Thee and Thy brother Balarama in all your infinite glory.

[*Enter Balarama. Akrura falls on Balarama's feet.*]

I saw you, my Lord as Sesha Naga, the foundation of the world. And your brother is truly Maha Vishnu—the light of lights! I am at peace of mind and all my fears are over. Come charioteer, Mathura awaits us.

END OF ACT 3 SCENE 1

ACT 3 SCENE 2

A Street Scene—Mathura

GOMATI. [*Comes in panting for breath.*] Sister Leela, I have been blessed today. I have seen them! I have seen them!

LEELA. What are you talking about? Who have you seen?

GOMATI. I have seen the inimitable pair from Vrindavan, Krishna and Balarama. The fair one, gentle and handsome, is Balarama. The tall dark one, the handsome prince, with a sky blue face, is Krishna. Thank God I have lived to see the day.

LEELA. Where are they? Are they coming this way?

GOMATI. They have just passed Chakori Bazaar. A large crowd is following them. Let us stand on those two rocks so that we may have a better view of the matchless divine pair.

LEELA. [*Holding Gomati's hands*] Come sister, let us stand on the highest steps of the pavilion. We will see them better from there.

FIRST SAGE. [*An old sage with a one-stringed instrument.*] Narayan! Narayan! Make way! Make way! The lord is coming this way. Make way for the lord and his brother Balarama.

[*The sage crosses the street and continues making the same pronouncement*]

FIRST MAN. Make way for Vrindavan's Kanhaya!

SECOND MAN. Make way for Murali Manohar, make way for Devaki-Nandan!

THIRD MAN. Make way for Balarama, the incarnation of Sheshu, the thousand-fanged serpent that holds the earth aloft.

VOICES. Shri Krishna ki jai! Shri Krishna ki jai!

[*The crowd comes into the street. They follow Krishna and Balarama.*]

SECOND SAGE. [*Garlanding Krishna and Balarama—with folded hands and addressing Krishna.*] Hail to Thee, Divine Master. Thou art the Light of the World. Thank you for blessing Mathura with your presence. Thank you for spreading your effulgent light on our city. Jai Krishna Hari! Jai Krishna Hari!

[*A blind man held by another walks to the centre of the stage.*]

FIRST MAN. Make way for the blind man! Let him see the Lord!

BLIND MAN. If only my eyes could see Thy divine form, Oh Lord, I'll be thrice blessed. Touch me, Oh Lord, so that I may feel Thy divine grace.

KRISHNA. [*Touches the blind man*] Open your eyes, Baba.

BLIND MAN. [*Opens his eyes, sees Krishna, and falls on his feet.*] My dear lord, you have always resided in my heart.

By seeing your lotus feet today I have fulfilled my life's goal. Oh, my Krishna Kanhaya, if after every agony come such soothing balms, let fate have its day!

CROWD. Shri Krishna ki jai! Murali Manohar ki jai!

[*A man carrying a tray of fruits enters. With him are two boys and a girl. All of them prostrate before Krishna.*]

POOR MAN. Oh, Shyam Sundar, Oh, dark handsome prince, I have been keeping these for you. My lord, all my poor family can give you is a plate of fruits. Forgive me, Oh Lord, for my small gift.

KRISHNA. Arise, my dear friend, arise! I bless you and your family for this magnificent gift. [*Eats an apple*] A leaf, a flower, a fruit is most welcome. If anything is given to me with love and devotion I accept joyfully.

[*The poor man and his family leave*; *enter Trivakra, a hunch-backed young woman.*]

SECOND MAN. Make way for Trivakra, the hunch-backed woman.

[*The crowd laughs.*]

TRIVAKRA. Let me see my Murali Manohar. Yes, I am ugly, I am thrice-crooked. Let me go!

SECOND MAN. Make room! Make room for Trivakra!

TRIVAKRA. Oh, my prince, in yellow and blue, I have been waiting for you for a long time.

[*Prostrates herself before Krishna*]

KRISHNA. Waiting for us? Who are you, my dear sister?

TRIVAKRA. I am just a crippled woman. Once, I was called Malini and now the folks call me Trivakra, the thrice crooked one. I don't mind. But they don't know what I have brought for you, my dear Govinda.

BALARAMA. Oh, I guess you have brought peda, Mathura's favourite sweetmeat!

TRIVAKRA. No, my dear Balarama, something unique!

KRISHNA. What is it?

TRIVAKRA. I am in charge of cosmetics and perfume in the royal household. I have been preparing these unguents especially for you. May I apply some of the cosmetics on you?

KRISHNA. Most certainly, my dear Malini!

TRIVAKRA. For you Shyam Sundar, this sandalwood paste, from my silver box. For your blue and yellow attire this perfume made from champa-chameli.

[*And turning towards Balarama*]

For you, handsome prince in blue, these scent and unguents made from the rarest flowers in Mathura.

BALARAMA. Oh, that's wonderful. I think I'll swoon with these delightful perfumes.

[*Trivakra prostrates on Krishna's feet.*]

KRISHNA. Arise Malini, my sweet sister, Trivakra is no more!

[*Trivakra raises herself—her hunchback has gone. The crowd is stunned by her change.*]

THIRD MAN. Shri Krishna ki jai! Balarama ki jai!

TRIVAKRA. [*Trivakra rises.*] I am nolonger thrice-crooked, I am now thrice-blessed!

[*Enter Prince Rukmi and Princess Rukmini. Three soldiers come blustering in.*]

FIRST SOLDIER. Leave the road at once! Make way! Make way! Make way!

SECOND SOLDIER. Clear thestreet! Bow to Maharaja Kamsa's guests Prince Rukmi and Princess Rukmini.

[*With the exception of Krishna and Balarama the rest clear the street.*]

FIRST SOLDIER. [*To Balarama and Krishna*] Why don't you two clear the streets?

[*Pushes Balarama but Balarama throws the soldier off the road.*]

PRINCE RUKMI. Do you know who I am? I am Rukmi, the Crown Prince of Vidarbha. You scoundrels, who do you think you are?

KRISHNA. We are cowherds from Vrindavan, Krishna and Balarama. We, too, are guests of Maharaja Kamsa. We have as much right as you have!

PRINCE RUKMI. Out of my way, you knaves. You scum of the earth, you will pay for your arrogance.

[*Pulls out his sword, but Balarama holds Rukmi's wrist and breaks the sword, he holds Rukmi's hand so hard that he begins to scream.*]

PRINCESS RUKMINI. [*To Balarama*] Oh, what have you done to my brother? Have you broken his hands?

[*The soldiers start moving to Rukmi.*]

Mighty Rukmi, do you need help to fight these two country cowherds?

[*The soldiers move towards Krishna and Balarama.*]

PRINCE RUKMI. [*To the soldiers*] Leave these country bumpkins alone. I'll find a suitable time and place to deal with them. Let us go.

[*All leave but Rukmini who looks at Krishna's face.*]

KRISHNA. [*Smiling*] Fair maid, is this unruly and unmannerly man, your brother?

[*Rukmini nods.*]

My dear Princess, royalty commands nobility and grace, and not demand brute force. I hope you will teach your brother some manners and etiquette.

PRINCESS RUKMINI. [*Pushes her way forward*] Let me go.

[*Turns towards Krishna and smiles*]

KRISHNA. Farewell princess, the cowherd will certainly meet you again!

THE CROWD. Shri Krishna ki jai! Shri Krishna ki jai! Balarama ki jai!

FIRST MAN. Here comes General Pradyota! I guess there's more trouble ahead.

SECOND MAN. Make way for the Andhaka chief! Make way for Maharaja Kamsa's general!

PRADYOTA. [*Addressing Balarama and Krishna*] I am the chief security officer of the royal palace. I am Pradyota, Chief of the Andhakas. Are you Chief Nand's sons, Krishna and Balarama?

KRISHNA. Yes, we are!

PRADYOTA. I have spent the whole morning in search of you esteemed guests of Maharaja Kamsa. Chief Nandji, your saintly father, has already arrived. May I have the pleasure of guiding you to our palace hospitality centre? The palace staff await your arrival.

KRISHNA. Thank you, General Pradyota, for your cheerful welcome. But we regret our inability to come with you. Our hospitality has already been taken care of. Tonight, we shall be the guests of our old friends in old Mathura. But tomorrow morning we shall make our rounds to the palace. Where shall we meet?

PRADYOTA. If you come to the sacrificial arena I shall show you the sacred bow.

KRISHNA. Yes, my dear general. Tomorrow we shall meet!

[*Pradyota and his retinue leave.*]

Balarama, you and I must leave now! Our hosts are waiting for us. Farewell, good people of Mathura.

FIRST MAN. Make way for Krishna and Balarama! Make way for Vrindavan Behari! Make way!

[*The crowd moves. Everyone leaves but the second sage.*]

SECOND SAGE. Oh, my Giridhari, my dear flute-player, today we have seen your divine majesty at work. Oh, Infinite Lord, tomorrow you meet the monster Maharaja Kamsa. Now that you have manifested yourself in finite form, I know you will protect the good, the virtuous and destroy the wicked and establish dharma again. Narayan! Narayan!

END OF ACT 3 SCENE 2

ACT 3 SCENE 3

Dhanuryajna—the Sacred Bow Festival: The Sacrificial Arena

[*A special pavilion is erected for the Dhanuryajna, the sacred bow festival. It is guarded by soldiers and security men. The pavilion is still closed to the public but three priests are around the sacred bow chanting their holy mantras. General Pradyota is sitting in one corner.*]

FIRST SOLDIER [*Comes dashing in to the room and gets General Pradyota's attention*] Greetings, my lord, I bring astounding news.

GENERAL PRADYOTA. Compose yourself, sit down!

[*The soldier sits.*]

What earth-shattering news do you bring?

FIRST SOLDIER. [*Rises once more*] My lord, the elephant has been tamed. It is a miracle!

GENERAL PRADYOTA. Which elephant? What are you talking about?

FIRST SOLDIER. Kuvalayapida the terrible, the most powerful elephant in the royal palace succumbed to the soothing words of the cowherd from Vrindavan.

FIRST PRIEST. The Master of the elephants couldn't subdue the angry elephant. The heavy ornamental gold chain broke into two and the elephant went charging wildly. The crowd screamed, ran helter-skelter, and the older cowherd moved to one side, but the dark handsome one, Krishna, got hold of the elephant's trunk, patted it, and spoke a few kindly words.

GENERAL PRADYOTA. Yes, that's astounding! And then what happened?

FIRST SOLDIER. The elephant extended his trunk and Krishna put his hand into its mouth. There was an ecstatic scream from the crowd. Someone started chanting: Jai Krishna, Shri Krishna ki jai. The crowd took it up and burst into a frenzy.

SECOND PRIEST. I think Krishna, the flute-bearer of Vrindavan, has a special gift with animals. Not only does he know how to enter the hearts of young maidens, he also knows how to calm and soothe animals. I think there's something divine about him.

GENERAL PRADYOTA. Yes, I think so too. All the stories we hear about his famous deeds must be true. I think he will change the course of destiny and make Vrindavan, Gokula and Mathura a better place. He must be coming to visit us soon.

[*The priests begin to pray. The doors are opened and the crowd come in.*]

TRIVAKRA. Gomati, did you hear joyous shout from the crowd?

GOMATI. Yes, Leela and I were moved to ecstasy. Leela

began saying: Jaya Jaya Nandnandan—Victory, Victory to the son of Nand. The crowd took it up. There were tears in my eyes.

LEELA. We are fortunate that we were born in this age.

[*Krishna and Balarama enter. The crowd shout Jaya Jaya Nandnandan.*]

CROWD. Jaya Jaya Jaya Nandnandan! Jai Krishna Hari!

GENERAL PRADYOTA. Welcome, Krishna and Balarama, welcome to our sacred pavilion!

KRISHNA. Thank you, general. We were looking forward to seeing the mysterious bow.

GENERAL PRADYOTA. Krishna, I have just heard about your encounter with the elephant. Congratulations! I am glad you are safe otherwise Maharaja Kamsa would blame me if anything went wrong with his honoured guests.

BALARAMA. Krishna, the enchanter of man and beast, has had a lot of experience dealing with wild and dangerous animals. His melodious music has soothed many a savage beast. Hastin, the dangerous bull, was so pacified that he joyfully allowed Krishna to ride on his back. Kaliya, the poisonous snake, was mesmerised by the divine Krishna, that she cheerfully accepted him to dance on her head.

KRISHNA. General, will you let us see the sacred bow?

GENERAL PRADYOTA. [*Addressing Krishna, Balarama and other guests from Vrindavan and Mathura*] Our honoured guests, Krishna and Balarama, and the good people of Vrindavan, I welcome you to see our sacred bow. It is a marvellous bow designed by artists, made by master craftsmen, and blessed by the gods, it is heavier than solid steel.

TRIVAKRA. When is the final ritual of shooting the arrow from the bow?

GENERAL PRADYOTA. It is on the last day of these joyful activities. The person whose arrow goes the longest distance is declared the winner and is proclaimed the hero of Dhanuryajna. It is one of the most coveted prizes of these festivities.

BALARAMA. We have never used a bow like this before. Our simple bows and arrows are made of wood and bamboo. It's light and easy to handle and we shoot wild animals with it.

TRIVAKRA. Krishna, are you proficient with bows and arrows?

KRISHNA. [*Laughing*] I am no archer, I am just a rustic, a simple cowherd, who loves to play his flute and take the cows to pasture. But I would like to shoot a few arrows on the last day.

[*Many people try to lift the bow but it won't budge an inch.*]

TRIVAKRA. [*Laughing*] I can't see how anyone can discharge arrows from this bow if they can't even pick it up. So far everyone in this room has failed. Balarama, why don't you try?

BALARAMA. No, ask Krishna to try first.

KRISHNA. General, may I have your permission to lift this bow and see how heavy it is?

GENERAL PRADYOTA. You are certainly welcome. But I must warn you that it is extremely heavy. Very few of our wrestlers, gymnasts and expert archers have been able to lift this sacred bow. But you may try.

KRISHNA. [*Examines the bow, feels the sides, and lifts it with ease.*] Well, this wasn't that heavy. But I must say it is very cumbersome.

TRIVAKRA. Why don't you try it?

GENERAL PRADYOTA. Go ahead! See if you can string an arrow to the bow.

KRISHNA. [*Krishna looks at the arrow, raises the bow, bends it and it breaks. There's a loud sound. The crowd is stunned.*] Oh, I didn't realize the frailty and weakness of this bow. Was it really made of solid wood by master craftsmen? General Pradyota, I am afraid you will have to make another one for the Dhanuryajna.

[*Trivakra falls on Krishna's feet. Other men and women fall prostrate on his feet.*]

CROWD. Shri Krishna ki jai! Krishna Kanhaya ki jai! Murali Manohar ki jai!

END OF ACT 3 SCENE 3

ACT 3 SCENE 4

The Wrestling Tournament—
The Wrestling Arena

[*The arena is all set for the great wrestling match, but it has not been open to the public yet. Maharaja Kamsa and his henchmen devise a strategy to finally destroy Krishna, Balarama and the Yadava chiefs.*]

MAHARAJA KAMSA. General Pradyota, why did you allow Krishna to handle the sacred bow?

GENERAL PRADYOTA. How could I stop him? Every archer, who enters the competition, has the right to test the bow. I only did my duty.

MAHARAJA KAMSA. Krishna grows arrogant and daring. By breaking the sacred bow he has committed a sacrilegious act. He continues humiliating and insulting our royal guests.

PRINCE VITRIGHNA. Yesterday, the older cowherd, Balarama, attacked Prince Rukmi and threw him out of the street, and the crowd roared in approval. This is an insult to royalty. Something must be done quickly to prevent another catastrophe.

MAHARAJA KAMSA. [*Gnashes his teeth*] Chanura, I depend on you.

CHANURA. Yes, my Lord. I shall do whatever you want me to do.

MAHARAJA KAMSA. Chanura, I know you are a professional, an honourable wrestler, but you have to make a supreme sacrifice for me.

CHANURA. Whatever your majesty wills, will be done. Just say the word!

MAHARAJA KAMSA. Lure Krishna to wrestle with you, break his bones, suffocate him, make an end of him!

[*Chanura nods.*]

GENERAL PRADYOTA. But the crowd will react vehemently. To let Chanura wrestle a young boy is against the rules of wrestling, against dharma. There will be an outcry.

MAHARAJA KAMSA. Prince Vitrighna, you take care of the unruly crowd. Chanura, I don't care how you do it, but do it!

CHANURA. Yes, my lord.

VITRIGHNA. Leave it to me, Maharaja. I have a thousand Magadhan soldiers, heavily armed, at my command. But may I suggest something else also?

MAHARAJA KAMSA. Yes, what is it?

PRINCE VITRIGHNA. I suggest Mushtika engage Balarama into a contest and make an end of that cowherd also!

MAHARAJA KAMSA. Mushtika, you and Chanur have an important duty to perform. [*Mushtika nods.*] General

Pradyota, I will be in my palace. Let me have the result of the contest as quickly as possible.

[*Maharaja Kamsa and his retiune leave. So does Prince Vitrighna, Chanura and Mushtika. General Pradyota remains.*]

GENERAL PRADYOTA. Guards, open the doors. Let the crowd come in an orderly fashion.

[*The crowd comes in and take their seats. They are followed by Nand, Krishna and Balarama.*]

CROWD. Jai Krishna Hari! Jai Krishna Hari! Jaya Jaya Nandnandan! Victory to the son of Nand!

[*Enter Prince Vitrighna, Princess Madhuri, Prince Rukmi and Princess Rukmini and their retinue.*]

GENERAL PRADYOTA. Welcome to our honourable guests: Prince Vitrighna, Princess Madhuri, Prince Rukmi and Princess Rukmini. Welcome to chief Nand, welcome to all the chiefs of Mathura, Gokula and Vrindavan. Welcome to Krishna and Balarama!

CROWD. Jaya Jaya Nandnandan! Jaya Jaya Nandnandan! Victory to the sons of Chief Nand.

[*Enter two conch-blowers. They blow the conches. Enter Mushtika and Chanura.*]

CROWD. Chanura ki jai! Mushtika ki jai.

FIRST CONCH-BLOWER. Meet Mushtika, the lion-hearted, a perfection of strength, the mountain-man, resplendent in the field of wrestling, the serpent of the ring! Mushtika!

CROWD. Mushtikaji ki jai! Mushtikaji ki jai.

[*Mushtika bows to the crowd.*]

SECOND CONCH-BLOWER. Now meet Chanura, the hero of Mathura, the slayer of dragons, hard as granite, fleet-footed, terrible as death, champion of champions, the invincible Chanura! Chanura!

CROWD. Chanura ji ki jai! Chanura ji ki jai!

GENERAL PRADYOTA. [*General Pradyota enters, raises his head and gets the crowd's attention.*] Today you will meet two of the greatest wrestlers in Bharat: Chanura and Mushtika. In a short while they will compete for a thousand gold crowns.

CROWD. Chanura ji ki jai! Mushtika ji ki jai!

GENERAL PRADYOTA. [*Pradyota raises his hand again. The crowd pays attention.*] Today we have wrestlers from other cities. Our great wrestlers throw an open challenge to anyone who wants to win the royal prize. If there's any, please come forward.

TRIVAKRA. Last night, we had cruel proof of Chanura's vicious strength. He transformed a wrestler into a pulp by breaking four of his ribs. Who would want to fight him?

CHANURA. [*Smiling*] Chief Nand, are those two boys your sons?

NAND. Yes, they are Balarama and Krishna.

CHANURA. I hear that Krishna is Vrindavan's giant and

Balarama's a fiery thunderbolt. Chief Nand, won't you let your sons compete? The spectators will be thrilled to see the display of their valour and strength. [*Laughing*] Come on, Chief, give the boys a chance.

NAND. No, I will not submit my sons to two towering giants like you. It is against all religious principles to match combatants of unequal age, size and strength. No, I will not allow it.

PRINCESS RUKMINI. I agree with Chief Nand. Krishna and Balarama are just boys. They are no match for Chanura or Mushtika.

PRINCE RUKMI. Why not? Let the boys go into the ring and show their might. [*Laughs*] These cowherds will find a lot of difference between young bulls in Vrindavan and real stalwarts in Mathura.

GOMATI AND LEELA. No! No! No! That won't be fair!

PRINCESS RUKMINI. I do not think breaking of ribs and maiming is a sport for decent folk. Bhaiya, do not let them engage these young men.

CHANURA. Have no fear, Princess, they will come to no harm. It's merely a sport. We shall try one fall only. Krishna, are you prepard to wrestle with me?

KRISHNA. [*Smile*] No, I am not afraid. You are a great wrestler and I am only a boy.

CHANURA. Yes, I know that. You are just a cowherd. All you love is milk and *dahi* and dance with the milk-maids.

AKRURA. Chanura, you are the master of *bahu-yuddha*, you are the king of the wrestlers. Balarama and Krishna are two young boys. Do not fight them. You break the sanctity of a great sport.

CHANURA. Krishna, are you afraid to wrestle with me? [*Krishna looks at his father, Nand.*] Why do you look at your father? You are a coward!

KRISHNA. I am no coward. I am Nandnandan.

[*He pulls of his head-dress, removes the ornaments on his clothes, and walks to the ring.*]

Chanura, I am ready.

CROWD. Jai Krishna Hari! Jai Krishna Hari!

Jaya Jaya Nandnandan! Jaya Jaya Nandnandan!

MUSHTIKA. [*Glares at Balarama*] Why do you keep your head down? Why don't we make our fight the curtain-raiser?

[*Balarama looks at Nand.*]

Stop looking at your father. Look at me! Are you also friendly with the girls, or are you just a fat little girl?

BALARAMA. You talk too much. My voice is in my arms. Come, you arrogant beast, show me your strength.

[*They fight.*]

MAYNA. Jai Hanuman! I hope the little strength I have would be trnsported to you, Krishna.

BALARAMA. [*Fights vigorously.*] Jai Bajrangbali ki!

SHALINI. God be with you Balarama! If I were an apsara I would tear his eyes.

[*Mushtika is thrown. Shouts.*]

CROWD. Balarama ki jai! Balarama ki jai! Vrindavan ki jai!

GENERAL PRADYOTA. That's enough! No, more, I pray.

BALARAMA. I have just begun general. That was the easiest of my tricks, a little more time, please!

GENERAL PRADYOTA. Mushtika, do you wish to continue?

SOLDIER. He does not speak, he has fainted. The fight is over for him!

CROWD. Jaya Nandnandan! Jaya Nandnandan!

CHANURA. [*Angry, leering at Krishna.*] Come, you cowherd. Now you wrestle with the great Chanura.

KRISHNA. [*Krishna smiles, slaps, his biceps and thighs.*] Come, Mathura's hero! Feel the embrace of the cowherd.

[*They fight, the crowd is silent. Chanura falls.*]

THE CROWD. Jaya Nandnandan! Murali Manohar ki jai.

[*Chanura rises.*]

CHANURA. This is your end. Say your prayers Krishna.

[*Krishna raises Chanura and throws him out of the ring. He falls with a thud.*]

CROWD. Jai Krishna! Shri Krishna!

TRIVAKRA. I knew Krishna wouldn't be defeated. He is a god. Jai Devaki-Nandan, Jai Nandnandan!

CROWD. Jai Devaki-Nandan, Jaya Nandnandan!

GENERAL PRADYOTA. [*Smiling*] And tomorrow to greater deeds! We shall see you all at the Dhanuryajna at the sacrificial arena.

CROWD. Balarama ki jai! Krishna ki jai! Devaki-Nandan ki jai! Nandnandan ki jai!

END OF ACT 3 SCENE 4

ACT 3 SCENE 5

Prison—Mathura

VASUDEVA. The eerie silence of this cell is like an abode in hell. Not even the guards will utter a word. They throw us meals like dumb animals. Why is there such a deathly silence?

DEVAKI. Nath, I am certain a storm is brewing in the palace and Maharaja Kamsa wants to keep us in the dark. May-be, our son Krishna is on his way to redeem us.

VASUDEVA. No, Devi, our son has forgotten us. Krishna is no longer our son. He is the son of Nand and Yashoda and the darling of the gopis of Gokula.

DEVAKI. How can you say that Nath? Isn't he our child? Did you not take him across the Yamuna?

VASUDEVA. Yes, Devi, that happened many, many years ago. Why do you keep tormenting yourself by thinking of him from morn to dusk? Leave him alone, this is all part—.

DEVAKI. All part of our karma! I know, that is what you will say.

VASUDEVA. Yes Devi, it is our karma. Maharaja Kamsa treats us as common criminals by putting us in and out of prison. How long do we have to be incarcerated in this horrible dungeon?

DEVAKI. Patience, Nath, patience! Have you already forgotten about our divine child? Do you remember how the waters parted so that you were able to cross the Yamuna safely?

VASUDEVA. Yes, my dear Devaki, I remember those sublime moments: they were full of mystery. As soon as the water subsided there was a flash of lightning and the bells began to peel loud and long, loud and long!

DEVAKI. And I waited patiently for you!

VASUDEVA. Yes, Devi, I remember. As I looked up I think I saw flying chariots with gods and goddesses. They showered flowers upon us and the Yamuna became a floral paradise. I heard them say again and again: Krishna! Krishna! Hare! Hare! Krishna! Krishna! Hare! Hare! It may seem strange and mysterious but that was a divinely poignant moment.

DEVAKI. The ways of the lord are infinite. Have faith Nath, have faith. Faith is divine, faith is like rain-clouds, hovering overhead, ready to give its life-giving showers when the moment is ripe. Come, Nath, faith and patience have been the virtues upon which we have leaned for so long. Let us not give up now. Let us pray.

[*Devaki and Vasudeva kneel down to pray—but only Devaki's voice can be heard.*]

Oh God! How much longer must we endure this pain and suffering? My Lord Shiva-Shankar, please send our son to redeem us. Oh Krishna, wherever Thou art, come to us now. Even if you are in the heavens burst upon us!

[*They remain—meditating. Voice can be heard—enter Krishna, Balarama and Akrura.*]

VASUDEVA. Who are you? How did you enter this forbidden cell? The guards keep a careful watch and every intruder is killed instantly. If they see you they will certainly punish you severely.

KRISHNA. You needn't fear mother. Do you know me ?

[*Devaki shakes her head.*]

I am Krishna.

DEVAKI. Krishna, my son, Krishna.

VASUDEVA. My son, Krishna, my son!

KRISHNA. Yes, mother, your Krishna and Balarama. We have come to relieve you and my father from the shackles of the tyrant. Mother, father, meet your eldest son Balarama.

DEVAKI. Balarama! Balarama!

[*Kneeling on the floor.*]

My lord, your devotees thank you for blessing us with our seventh and eighth sons: Balarama and Krishna!

VASUDEVA. Balarama! Balarama!

[*They embrace each other.*]

Krishna! Krishna!

[*Both hold their mother and father's shoulders.*]

Shri Akrurji, may god bless you for all that you have done for us.

DEVAKI. Guruji, thank you for bringing both our sons.

[*Kneels.*]

VASUDEVA. But how can we defeat Maharaja Kamsa, my son?

DEVAKI. Maharaja Kamsa has thousands of rakshasas. The guards are heavily armed and they are at the tyrant's beck and call every moment of the day and night. What will you do?

AKRURA. Your Majesties, have faith in Balarama and Krishna. They have a special divinity in them. They have already been acclaimed heroes by the people of Mathura.

DEVAKI. But how can they confront Kamsa's terrible death-dealing warriors? How can our two young sons match their physical prowess?

AKRURA. Devaka's noble daughter Devaki, your sons are two illustrious souls. Krishna has already pacified the angry elephant and Balarama has vanquished Mushtika, the powerful wrestler.

VASUDEVA. Yadavji, did you say that Balarama defeated Mushtika, the mighty court wrestler?

AKRURA. Yes, noble sire, and Krishna made short-shift of the terrible monster, Chanur.

[*Maharaja Kamsa, soldiers and guards enter the prison*]

MAHARAJA KAMSA. Krishna, where are you?

KRISHNA. I am here, Krishna, your *kaal* your death.

MAHARAJA KAMSA. [*Laughs hysterically.*] So you are Krishna! So you are the eighth son of Devaki. How fortunate have I been to get you come right into my hands. You are a prey that I have hunted for a long time. Each time my spies have cornered you, you have escaped.

KRISHNA. [*Smiling*] They say I am illusive, like a shadow darting from the earth to the heavens.

MAHARAJA KAMSA. Come, Krishna, wrestle with the mighty Kamsa. I shall kill you with my bare hands.

KRISHNA. Maharaja Kamsa, your tyranny has shaken the foundations of the earth. You have terrified everyone: Indralok shivers, the earth quivers, and the world trembles with your sin. You are not fit to be a king.

[*Maharaja Kamsa moves towards Krishna. Devaki falls on Kamsa's feet.*]

DEVAKI. My brother, my lord, spare Krishna. He is your nephew.

MAHARAJA KAMSA. Out of my sight, you traitor! Once I have dispensed with Krishna, you and Vasudeva will meet similar fate.

KRISHNA. Mother, don't plead with him anymore. He has no remorse he has usurped his father's throne, imprisoned my dear grandfather.

MAHARAJA KAMSA. Enough of your speech. Come little cowherd, this is your end.

[*Enter Nand, Yashoda, Gopas and Gopis and Narad Muni; Yashoda runs towards Krishna.*]

YASHODA. My son! my son!

MAHARAJA KAMSA. Ecstasy, ecstasy! So this is the romance of the cowherd family. Guards kill everyone of these cowherds. Come, you cowherds, you milker of cows. I shall kill you one by one. Wait! I want a larger audience. I want them to see how the mighty Kamsa will crush their little darling.

[*Yashoda falls on Kamsa's feet.*]

YASHODA. No! No! No!

MAHARAJA KAMSA. Go out of my sight you cowering woman. Krishna, do you see this sword. No one ever escapes it. You cowherds watch!

[*Kamsa comes towards Krishna with his sword.*]

This stab will be fatal, this will be the end of you.

[*Krishna holds Kamsa's hand and takes away his sword—and throws him to the ground.*]

KRISHNA. Here, you proud and haughty tyrant.

[*Kamsa falls on the ground and Krishna makes an end of him with his bare hands; Krishna picks up the royal crown; Nand and Yashoda, Devaki and Vasudeva move towards Krishna.*]

CROWD. Jai Krishna Hari! Jai Krishna Hari! Jai Krishna Hari! Jai Krishna Hari!

[*Enter King Ugrasena and guards.*]

KRISHNA. [*Walking towards King Ugrasena*] My Lord, great King Ugrasena, my grandfather, I have rid the world of one great evil. Maharaja Kansraj is no more!

[*Placing the crown on King Ugrasena's head.*]

Great monarch, this crown belongs to you. May you rule wisely, long be your reign!

NARAD MUNI. Narayan! Narayan! Narayan! The prophecy has been fulfilled.

Yada yada hi dharmasya
Glanir bhavati bharata
Abhyutthanam adharmasya
Tadatmanam srijamy aham.

The Lord said that whenever and wherever there is a decline in righteousness and a rise of adharma or evil, my spirit will arise on earth.

Say: Shri Krishna ki jai! Sri Krishna ki jai!

THE END

GLOSSARY

AKASH VANI: Literally—a voice from the sky. Here, it is a prophetic voice from the heavens.

ASHWAMEDHA: This ceremony is usually performed by kings for obtaining heirs for their kingdoms. A white horse is selected for the function. It is fed for three days, set free to wander at will for a year, and then sacrificed.

APSARA: A celestial nymph. They live in Indralok, Indra's heaven. Celebrated among apsaras are Urvasi, Menaka and Rambha.

BABA: Father, priest, or an affectionate way of addressing an older man.

BAHEN: Sister.

BETI: Daughter.

BHAIYA: Brother.

BRIJLAL: Son of Vraj. Vraj was the kingdom of Mathura in which Lord Krishna was born.

DEVARSHI: Refers to Narad Muni, the wandering sage. He was the chief of the sages.

DEVI: An angel, religious, devout female. An affectionate way of addressing one's wife.

DHARMA: A divinely established law of the universe. The term applies to various aspects of moral and spiritual value.

DIDI: Elder sister.

GANGA: The most sacred river in India, regarded as a celestial goddess. The Ganga is said to have emerged from Vishnu's feet and Shiva took the stream upon his matted hair lest the mighty force should destroy the earth.

GHAT: It is a sacred area close to river banks. These holy places are used for ablutions, bathing and prayer. Saints, sages, and the Hindu devotees gather here for religious occasions. A cremation ghat is usually at the banks of rivers.

GOPAS (m) GOPIS (f): The term is specifically used to describe village maidens or cow-girls and village lads or cowherds of Vrindavan. Gopas and Gopis were friends and playmates of Lord Krishna.

HARI: God, redeemer. A common name of divinity such as Shiva, Vishnu, Mahesha and Rama and Krishna.

JAI HANUMAN: Victory to Hanuman. Hanuman was the god of the wind. He is known as the messenger of Rama. Many Hindus worship Hanuman as a God. He is the God of strength, might and power.

JAYA NANDNANDAN: Victory of the son of Nand. Nandan is son.

KAAL: Death, personified.

KARMA: It generally refers to actions and deeds committed in the past. Every action has a reaction. It directs how the individual soul moves from one birth to another.

KOEL: The Indian cuckoo bird. A bird with a sweet voice.

LADDOO: A very popular Indian sweetmeat made from chick pea flour and clarified butter and sugar.

LOTA: It is a brass, bronze, silver or gold container in which Hindus carry water for worship.

MAHARAJ KANS KI JAI: Victory to Maharaja Kamsa.

MAKKHAN: Butter, clarified butter or cream.

NAMASKAR/NAMASTE: Greetings.

NAND GAON: The place of Nand.

NAND LAL: The son of Nand.

NARAYAN! NARAYAN!: One of the names of the Lord. Devotees chant the name constantly.

NATH: An affectionate way a wife addresses her husband.

OM HARI OM: The names of the lord. Devotees chant. Om refers to the omnipresent, omniscient, omnipotent god.

PANDIT/PUROHIT: Priest.

PEDA: A popular sweetmeat of Mathura—it's made from milk and cream.

PEEPAL: The holy fig tree.

POOTRA: Son.

PRADHAN MANTRI: The Chief Minister—Prime Minister.

PRANAAM: Greetings.

PRASAD: Divine offering—usually fruit, nuts or milk preparations.

RAKSHAS: Demon or demoness.

RAM/RAMACHANDRA: He was the seventh incarnation of God Vishnu and manifested Himself in Treta Yuga (Age). Lord Krishna was the eighth incarnation of Vishnu and he manifested Himself in Dwapar—an age after Rama.

ROTI: Unleavend Indian bread—usually made from wheat and corn.